THE POEM'S HEARTBEAT

Books by Alfred Corn

POETRY

Contradictions

Stake: Poems 1972–1992

Present

Autobiographies: Poems

The West Door

Notes from a Child of Paradise

The Various Light

A Call in the Midst of the Crowd: Poems

All Roads at Once

FICTION

Part of His Story

NON-FICTION

The Metamorphoses of Metaphor: Essays in Poetry and Fiction

Incarnation: Contemporary Writers on the New Testament

The Poem's Heartbeat: A Manual of Prosody (1997)

The Poem's Heartbeat

A Manual of Prosody

ALFRED CORN

Copper Canyon Press
Port Townsend, Washington

The Poem's Heartbeat was originally published by Story Line Press, 1997.

Copper Canyon Press is in residence at Fort Worden State Park in Port Townsend, Washington, under the auspices of Centrum. Centrum is a gathering place for artists and creative thinkers from around the world, students of all ages and backgrounds, and audiences seeking extraordinary cultural enrichment.

LIBRARY OF CONGRESS CATALOGING-IN-PUBLICATION DATA

Corn, Alfred, 1943–

The poem's heartbeat: a manual of prosody / Alfred Corn.

p. cm.

"The Poem's Heartbeat was originally published
by Story Line Press, 1997"—T.p. verso.

Includes bibliographical references and index.

ISBN 978-1-55659-281-2 (pbk.: alk. paper)

1. English language—Versification.   2. Poetics.
3. English language—Rhythm.   I. Title.

PE1505.C67 2008

808.1—dc22   2008014591

3 5 7 9 8 6 4 2

FIRST PRINTING

COPPER CANYON PRESS

Post Office Box 271

Port Townsend, Washington 98368

www.coppercanyonpress.org

for my students

ACKNOWLEDGMENTS

W.H. Auden, "If I Could Tell You" and excerpt from "His Excellency" from *W.H. Auden: Collected Poems,* edited by Edward Mendelson. Copyright 1945 by W.H. Auden. Copyright 1976 by Edward Mendelson, William Meredith, and Monroe K. Spears, Executors of the Estate of W.H. Auden. Used by permission of Random House, Inc., and Faber and Faber, Ltd.

Emily Dickinson, excerpts from "Those – dying then," and "Because I could not stop for Death –" from *The Complete Poems of Emily Dickinson,* edited by Thomas H. Johnson. Copyright 1951, 1955, 1979, 1983 by the President and Fellows of Harvard College. Reprinted by permission of the publishers and the Trustees of Amherst College.

Robert Graves, excerpt from "The Persian Version" from *The Collected Poems of Robert Graves.* Copyright 1975 by Robert Graves. Reprinted with the permission of Carcanet Press, Ltd.

R.S. Gwynn, excerpt from "Release" from *No Word of Farewell: Selected Poems 1970–2000.* Copyright 2000 by Story Line Press. Reprinted with the permission of the author.

Marilyn Hacker, excerpt from "Going Back to the River" from *Going Back to the River.* Copyright 1990 by Marilyn Hacker. Reprinted by permission of Frances Collin, Literary Agent.

Louis MacNeice, excerpt from "The Sunlight in the Garden" from *Selected Poems.* Copyright 1990 by Wake Forest University Press. Reprinted with the permission of David Higham Associates, Ltd.

Marianne Moore, excerpt from "The Steeple-Jack" from *Collected Poems of Marianne Moore.* Copyright 1935 by Marianne Moore, renewed 1963 by Marianne Moore and T.S. Eliot. Used with the permission of Viking Penguin, a division of Penguin Group (USA), Inc., and Faber and Faber, Ltd.

Contents

Preface

I sometimes teach prosody in graduate or undergraduate courses and have been perplexed by the problem of finding a textbook to assign for them. Many good books on meter and rhyme have been written, but most are out of print. Of those in print, some provide only an introduction to the subject (or treat only one aspect of it), some are spoiled by misinformation, and others begin immediately at a level too advanced for the beginner. What's really needed is a study that assumes no knowledge of meter on the part of the reader but then provides accurate information. An advanced subcategory of the study of prosody is *verseform* (for example, the sonnet and the villanelle), and two excellent introductions to verseforms are already available: John Hollander's *Rhyme's Reason* (Yale University Press) and Lewis Turco's *The New Book of Forms* (University Press of New England). This book doesn't, therefore, deal with verseforms exhaustively; but it does introduce the concept and discuss at length verseforms that poets writing in English have most often used.

My project is to introduce traditional English-language prosodic practice and then progress to fairly advanced levels of competence in it. The bibliography will offer readers a chance to carry their investigation of the subject further—after all, you can spend a lifetime exploring prosodic questions in English-language poetry alone. The goal here, though, is to provide answers to questions most often asked about prosody—not only for the reader uncertain how to hear or perform poems written in meter, but also for the poet attempting to use meter and rhyme as compositional resources.

Since the appearance of modernism in the 1910s and 1920s, poems written in English have more often than not dispensed with regular meter and rhyme—though it's also true that there never was a decade in the twentieth century when serious poets were not writing and publishing poems using traditional meters. In any case, after 1940, less attention was paid to prosody, with the result that few teachers of literature or practicing poets have more than a general understanding of it. The resource of meter has become much less available for contemporary poetry, obviously, but, besides that, there's another problem: contemporary readers are no longer able to follow all the intentions of poets from earlier periods. If we're not quite sure how Donne's "A Valediction Forbidding Mourning" was meant to sound, can we really pretend to have understood the poem? Certainly not all of it—a fact that ought to give us pause. To return to the present, let's acknowledge that contemporary poems are most often written in unmetered (and unrhymed) lines. All right, but do we have any notion of how *they* are meant to sound? We can begin to tackle that question, I think, only after we've understood traditional prosody. Too often these questions are bounced back and forth with simpleminded vehemence instead of objective argument. This book will, toward the end, take up the topic of what's usually called *free verse*—not to dismiss it, but to understand its relationship to traditional metrical practice. I hope to discuss the subject with more clarity than has been done before—and possibly even with humor, which

(Marianne Moore says in "The Pangolin") "saves a few steps, it saves years."

In conclusion, I would like to make grateful acknowledgment to students in the prosody classes I taught in the Writing Division of the School of the Arts at Columbia University in the years 1993–2001. The following chapters were developed in that context, and I received useful responses from a number of class members concerning the exposition of topics in meter, and patience from all as early drafts of each chapter were offered as the launching deck for discussion. I would also like to thank Grace Schulman for reading the first version of the book and making suggestions. Christopher Corwin offered encouragement throughout the writing of this book and kindly volunteered assistance in preparing the manuscript for publication, for which I am expressly grateful.

A.C.

Introduction

The art or study of versification is called *prosody,* the anglicized form of the Latin word *prosodia,* itself derived from the Greek *prosoide,* "a song with accompaniment." The derivations tell us that poets have traditionally taken for granted a strong connection between two cooperating arts based on the auditory sense. Greek poems were apparently always set to music, and the same is true for many ballads and poems in Western literature. Latin poems, though, were generally conceived as works independent of music, and that has been the rule for the greatest number of poems in our tradition after the classical period.

Even so, the connection still exists in our minds; otherwise, why would the adjective "musical" be so often applied to poems as a term of praise? Objectively considered, the two arts are quite different, and yet both involve hearing, just as they both require a given quantity of performance time in order to be perceived: you can't hear a sonata or read a poem instantaneously. What a poet expects you to hear is not much like the auditory stimulus a composer provides, but both poet and composer expect you to *hear.* And since time must elapse during the experience of hearing music or reading poetry, both arts use duration as one of their expressive resources.

Suppose we reflect a moment on the dimension of passing time that both music and poetry require. Duration that is unmarked or unmeasured is too vague to carry any precise meaning. If you find yourself in a windowless room without a watch, it's difficult to know how much time passes while you're there. Left in the dark about duration, you will find it difficult to assign a meaning to your stay in that windowless room: is it an all-too-brief retreat, or a long, painful incarceration? Maybe we can begin now to see why free-floating, unmarked time is a poor resource for the artist. Once a principle of measure is brought in, though, both music and poetry can draw on a wide range of expressive possibilities; and how poetry does so is one of the topics we will be looking at in the following chapters.

Granted the resemblance of poetry and music just outlined, we ought to reflect a moment on their differences. Music consists of a series of notes at assigned pitches sounded at designated intervals of time. Poetry prescribes the pitch of its component sounds not at all; different persons performing a poem aloud will use different pitches as they read it. There may be similarities in the *relative* distribution of high and low vocal pitches in these performances because various readers will nevertheless all base their recitations on the shared pitch-based intonational patterns of ordinary speech; but the poem text will not specify exact pitches for the words being read. The range of possible pitch variation is wide and depends on conscious or unconscious choices made by the person reading the poem. Since poets have only a limited control over pitch even when it is relative, they rely on it very little as an expressive resource.

Both poetry and music use accents to divide passing time into measurable units, but music provides a precise notation of that division in a way that poetry does not. In Western music, duration is marked by a series of equal units called *beats,* with a fixed number of these for each bar, the first beat (or *downbeat*) of each bar normally the strongest. Poetry's equivalent of musical beat is based on the variable energy required to articulate syllables of each word, and the regular recurrence of verbal *accent* (or *stress*) that falls on some of these syllables. Just as music is divided into a series of bars, poems are divided into a series of lines, each line (in traditional practice) containing an assigned number of stresses. Poetry does not, however, specify that the strongest accent in a line is the first. The relative strength of stresses in a line varies according to a number of factors, some having to do with the sound of individual words, others with the line's conceptual and emotional content.

A composer of music notates the number of beats per bar in the first bar of the composition, but poets never provide any separate notation of recurrent stresses apart from the line divisions; they assume that readers have learned the artistic conventions indicating where stresses should fall in each line. In poetry, rhythmic notation is fused with the actual words of poems themselves—which is why novices have trouble determining the governing rhythmic pattern. With practice, though, a reader is able to determine the overall meter of a poem usually after examining no more than two or three of its lines.

Music appeals to the ear through the play of varying pitch, through its rhythm, through the simultaneous sounding of more than one pitch (that is, harmony) and through the various timbres of the musical instruments or voices performing it. Since it is written for and read by a single voice, poetry offers no equivalent to harmony, nor does it use timbre as an expressive resource. Even though the vocal timbre of particular readers may contribute to the overall effect when a poem is read, this purely performative dimension can't be foreseen or prescribed by the poet. What poetry has instead of timbre is an appeal to the ear based on the interplay between vowels and consonants and their noticeable recurrence. (This aspect of poetic sound falls only marginally within the study of prosody, however, which is primarily concerned with the regulation of rhythmic accent.)

I hope it's now clear at least that, even aside from the issue of poetry's having conceptual content based on verbal communication, at the level of sound alone, the differences between poetry and music outweigh the similarities. That is why it is really misleading to use "musical" as a term of praise in poetry. Poetry has its own way of addressing the ear, and to praise that accurately we might speak instead of "effective sound" or "expressive rhythm" or "rich verbal texture." Vague or downright inaccurate as a descriptive term, "musical" is nevertheless brief and easy, so we'll probably continue to find it in critical journalism about poetry. Music and poetry do (in different ways) share a concern for rhythm, certainly; and the study of rhythm is the substance of prosody, which we turn to as we leave the topic of music.

Well then, what is *rhythm?* It is the general term we use to describe the patterning of accents (or beats or stresses) in time. It comes from the Greek word *rhythmos,* "measured motion," derived ultimately from a verb meaning "to flow." To experience rhythm, the ear must hear a recurrent sequence of accents at predictable intervals. For many reasons, human beings find this experience pleasurable and deeply engaging. Why? Partly because the principle of regular recurrence is found in nonartistic contexts as well, some of these primary in the formation of consciousness. Before an infant is born it develops a sense of hearing, and the first thing it hears is the heartbeat of the mother—a heartbeat perceived in a regularly recurring sequence. The steady rhythm of the mother's daily walk must also be experienced by the child as a physical sensation of gentle rocking to and fro. Eventually the child develops its own heartbeat, in counterpoint to the mother's. At birth, another primary rhythm is established, the intake and exhalation of breath. When the child begins to see, visual equivalents of rhythm emerge: the regular alternation of night and day; a series of steps from the ground floor up to the next level; the regularly repeating pattern on printed textiles or wallpaper.

As adults we are at least partly conscious of all sorts of sonic and visual rhythms at many junctures in our lives. Given room to walk without hindrance, we naturally fall into a precise rhythm as we move through space. We observe waves breaking on the shore of large bodies of water, and we note high and low tides in the ocean. We watch the moon rise and fall and move through several phases in a single month, before the same cycle begins again. Each year we experience the turnover of four seasons in a dependable sequence. In sports like rowing or running, children's games like jump rope, in dancing, in sexual relations, in singing or playing an instrument, we respond to rhythmic directives. If we are scientists, we observe and quantify rhythms at the subatomic level all the way up to the operation of the solar system and the interaction of galaxies throughout the universe. If we are painters, we may use regular rhythm as a design element in our paintings. And if we are poets, we will write poetry that draws on the human sense of rhythm to achieve an expressivity that we have felt intuitively.

When our sense of rhythm is developed, it becomes more

subtle. The absolutely regular insistence of a metronome or textile loom is not a pleasurable experience if it goes on for more than, say, fifteen seconds. For an artist, rhythm arises from the tension between regularity and irregularity, monotony and variety. Just as the predictable recurrence in pattern is a pleasure, departures from it also give pleasure, particularly when the departure has an aesthetic motive, when it adds to the "information" we are receiving. The play of regular against irregular rhythm is one of the most important expressive resources available to a poet. It's true that speech is finally too volatile ever to be perfectly quantified, but poets and metric theorists in the Western tradition have over the centuries developed a system of measurement and description that allows us to apply a kind of yardstick to poetic speech and so begin to analyze its rhythmic effects.

We should keep in mind, though, that these principles are not purely linguistic, not based solely on scientific measurement of what we hear. They are a set of artistic conventions that not only describe but also *shape* the spoken performance of particular poems. Unless we know what those conventions are, we can't fully grasp every metrical nuance active in a poem. Part of prosodic skill depends on attentive hearing, but another part of it is based on considerations that aren't strictly audible. To use prosody in reading poems, we have to hear what is audible, certainly, but we must also apply prosodic conventions not entirely governed by the sound of ordinary, unliterary speech. Application of these conventions might be described as "hearing with the inner ear," a kind of hearing that you will gradually acquire as you examine (and perform aloud) examples cited for study in the following chapters. Since by now you are probably impatient to get started, let's begin by examining *verbal accent,* the stress placed on syllables and words, singly and in cooperation, so that we can see exactly how poetic rhythm is achieved.

THE POEM'S HEARTBEAT

1. Line and Stress

A term often used to describe poetry written with meter is *verse,* which comes from Latin *versus,* meaning "turned around or turned back." Poetry, whether metered or not, is written in a series of lines whose words move from left to right, continue until the poet decides the line is complete, and then return to the left-hand margin to begin anew. This is the "turning" signified in the word "verse." Of course, prose must also return to the left-hand margin in order to fit normal page format, but the decision about where it does turn back is made by the typesetter, not the author. In the modern period, we've seen the development of a form called "prose poetry," which dispenses with the traditional poetic decision about where lines end; in all other cases, dividing the poem into definite units or *lines* is part of the task of composition.

Why *is* poetry written in lines? For one thing, they provide visual reinforcement for the fact that the poem is divided into a series of rhythmically measured units. This reinforcement isn't, however, visual only. Isolating a fragment of text in a line leads us to read it with more rhythmic insistence than we would if the fragment were simply part of a larger, unbroken sentence. When a poem is parceled out in a series of manageable units, we tend to read it more slowly; the slower reading helps us discover, in the limited compass of each line, engaging rhythmic qualities. Of course, those latent rhythmic qualities must actually be present; otherwise the special opportunity and expectation offered by lineation will go begging. Dividing a text into a series of lines that have no palpable rhythmic energy only highlights that lack and provokes a feeling of disappointment. (Prose poems, since they dispense with the assistance of lines, have to deploy special syntactic energies in order to charge their texts with the rhythmic intensity associated with poetry.)

Apart from helping us discover the special rhythmic potential of a text, writing in lines suggests that the single line of a poem is itself interesting as a *unit*, over and above its function as one in a series of stepping-stones composing the poem. In the very best poems, each separate line strikes us as a special entity, something with its own living character, worth examining in isolation from the rest. Consider this line

Grace was in all her steps, heav'n in her eye,

from Milton's *Paradise Lost* (Book VIII). Even though the line doesn't complete Milton's sentence and can be fully understood only in context, it has nevertheless an interesting rhythm, syntactic tension, and metaphoric power that can be independently enjoyed. (One of the reasons metrical theorists refer to Milton so often is that almost every line of his by itself repays study.) When beginning writers are trying to determine whether their abilities reside more in poetry than in prose, one quick litmus test to apply is to ask themselves this question: "Am I interested in conveying a truth that is broad and seamless as a mural or tapestry; or am I interested in conveying a vision that is really a series of intuitive and technical lightning flashes?" If the latter description of the writer's task is the one that most attracts you, then poetry is the better fit. As soon as the question is settled, all you have to do then is go on to produce complete and unified poems in which every line contains its depth charge of technical/intuitive insight. A tall order? Yes, as tall as Mount Parnassus, to whose slopes many are called but few are chosen.

One qualification needs to be introduced here: Marianne Moore said that for her the unit was not the line, but the syntactic unit as marked by punctuation (Grace Schulman, "Conversation with Marianne Moore," *Quarterly Review of Literature* 16 [1969], pp. 162–163). When we look at her poems, we can see what she meant. Given lines are often syntactic fragments ending in "the" or "a," and sometimes a line's end word is broken in half, with a hyphen connection to the word's next syllable, which opens the following line. In cases like these, the line reads as anything but a complete unit, an approach that goes against the grain of traditional prosody. It constitutes a notable element in the modernist, experimental aspect of Moore's work, which explores the tension between the visual aspect of verse lines and purely phrasal units of discourse. Moore does not, however, always take this special approach to lineation, given that many of her poems consist of perfectly viable separate (and even rhymed) lines, according to traditional metrical practice.

The word *line* comes from the Latin *linea,* itself derived from the word for a thread of linen. We can look at the lines of poetry as slender compositional units forming a weave like that of a textile. Indeed, the word "text" has the same origin as the word "textile."

It isn't difficult to compare the compositional process to weaving, where thread moves from left to right, reaches the margin of the text, then shuttles back to begin the next unit. This motion—a slow progress from left to right, followed by a quick left reversal before beginning again—is part of both writing and reading, a kind of pendulum swing intrinsic to the experience of poetry. Since the oscillation occurs more times per minute than in the parallel experience of reading prose, it contributes to the hypnotic quality of poetry. What may or may not be obvious is that poetry has never fully disengaged itself from its associations with shamanism; the poet, like the shaman, has mastered certain techniques—rhythmic, performative, imagistic, metaphoric—that summon the unconscious part of the mind, so that, in this dreamlike state between waking and sleeping, we may discover more about our thoughts and feelings than we would otherwise be able to do.

One compositional issue that must be decided by the poet is the question of whether a given line is to be *end-stopped*—that is, concluded with strong punctuation like the period, question mark, exclamation point, colon, semicolon, dash, or comma. When it is end-stopped, the line of course corresponds to a single syntactic unit. Shakespeare's Sonnet 40 begins with four consecutive end-stopped lines:

> Take all my loves, my love; yea, take them all.
> What hast thou then more than thou hadst before?
> No love, my love, that thou mayst true love call;
> All mine was thine before thou hadst this more.

The other possibility is that a line ends without any punctuation at all, so that the reader continues on to the next without a pause, the two lines being joined in one syntactic unit. In the same sonnet a few lines farther on, this also happens:

> But yet be blam'd, if thou thyself deceivest
> By willful taste of what thyself refusest.

The second line is end-stopped, but not the first, and therefore any performance of the lines has to mark the difference. Quite a long pause occurs after the second line, but almost none at all after the first. Because this difference obviously affects the rhythmic flow of the lines in question, the poet must incorporate that difference into the array of significant sonic resources at work in the poem. We will see, a bit farther on, how this can be done.

Writing a line without end-stopping is called *runover* or *enjambment* (from the French *enjambement,* which includes the word *jambe,* i.e., "leg"). Both "runover" and "enjambment" are terms with metaphoric resonances, which may help explain how poets use them. "Runover" suggests something like impetuosity that can't be contained within a prescribed unit, that chafes against maintenance of a rhythmic pattern incorporating built-in pauses at prescribed intervals. "Enjambment," because of its etymology, summons up the image of a hiker taking a long step between two separate footholds—the end of one line and the beginning of the next, almost as though the step taken is something like a stretch. We find a hint of this in the following enjambment:

> And move with a stilted stride
> To the land of sheer horizon, hunting Traherne's
> *Sensible emptiness,*...
>
> RICHARD WILBUR, "A World Without Objects Is a
> Sensible Emptiness"

The impression of a step taken across a gap is easily perceptible between lines one and two, and, moreover, the sensation of emptiness in that gap is reinforced by the enjambment between lines two and three.

As an example of the metaphoric suggestion available in the term *runover,* look at these lines (from *Paradise Lost,* Book VI, ll. 488–491):

> Such implements of mischief as shall dash
> To pieces, and o'erwhelm whatever stands
> Adverse, that they shall fear we have disarmed
> The thunderer of his only dreaded bolt.

All these lines are runovers (that is, enjambed) except the last, which is end-stopped. We should consider how much of the expressive energy of the lines arises from the sentence's impetuous refusal to contain itself within the prescribed unit. The portrait of furious energy in an unbridled adversarial stance smashing resistance into pieces is powerfully rendered here, not only by the rhythmic energy of the lines but also by the runovers' breaking of lines into pieces of syntax rather than a neat division into syntactic units with end-stopping. Do we need to be told that the speaker of these lines is Satan, also traditionally know as "the Adversary"? Between lines two and three, an enjambment stretches across the gap, making a palpable addition to our sense of Satan's adversarial stance, where the leftward "turning" of verse symbolizes his turning against God, though of course, it is the heavenly army that is described here as "adverse" from Satan's point of view. Finality comes only with the period after the word "bolt"—the lightning bolt to be stolen from "the thunderer," which is the Judeo-Christian God fused with his classical predecessor Zeus. The situation described here and the metrical means reinforcing it are extreme, but then so is Milton's subject. Poets with more modest subjects and aims than Milton's have even so relied on enjambment's unimpeded movement from line to line as one of their expressive resources. A runover that is purely accidental—one that lacks an expressive justification—amounts to a (perhaps minor) technical failure; unless, of course, the poem is, like one of Marianne Moore's, developing a tension between the syntactical compositional units and line division.

Most poems have traditionally been divided into lines all nearly of the same length because they correspond to the yardstick of auditory measure that meter provides. The effort to apply metrical norms to texts not written in lines—whether prose or "prose poems"—is practically meaningless. This fact may lead us to wonder whether dividing a text into lines without making those lines metrical is *also* a meaningless endeavor; that is one of the questions that will be considered in the chapter on what is usually called *free verse*. But we must first understand what meter in itself is before we can see how it is bound to the concept of line.

Meter (from Latin *metrum,* "measure") is simply a controlled pattern of auditory stimuli established in the opening lines of a verse composition, a pattern that the audience immediately hears and thereafter expects to continue hearing (with some variation) throughout the work. The most common definition of poetry is "a literary work composed in meter"; for meter to be unmistakably perceptible, the verse composition must be divided in lines so that a recurrent pattern can be located and performed.

Meter can be based on one of several auditory characteristics of language, but poetry in English has, since the Anglo-Saxon period, employed almost universally a meter based on verbal stress or "accent." *Accent* is often used to characterize variant speech patterns within one language as an "English accent" or a "Texas accent," but in discussions of meter it simply means the stress placed on individual syllables, the intensity with which those syllables are pronounced. Another word for *accent* or *stress* in this sense is *ictus,* which is Latin for "stroke" or "beat." All of these are synonyms for a brief but strong auditory stimulus readily perceived. In spoken English, each syllable receives weaker or stronger stress as a regular phonemic feature of the language. Stress in single syllables is perceptible as such by one or more of the following sound characteristics: amplitude (or loudness); length; pitch differential; and energy of articulation. The vocal apparatus, in order to produce stronger stress, sends more air through the vocal cords and powers it with more exertion in the diaphragm, the muscle in the thorax that controls breathing. Louder syllables, longer syllables, syllables higher in pitch, and syllables more carefully pronounced will all be perceived as having more stress or a stronger accent. In the phrase "Dick and Jane and Liz and Meg," stress is stronger on the proper names than on the connectives, the result of probably all four of the sound characteristics listed above.

Notice that every syllable we speak must receive *some* stress, in order to be audible; but certainly some syllables have stronger stress than others, and this comparative difference is the basis for meter in English. It can't be said too often that English meter is based on *relative* differences between the stress placed on a syllable and the syllables coming directly before and after it. This fact will become clearer when we look at specific examples, but we are already aware of relative stress differences (at least unconsciously) in our production and hearing of ordinary speech. For example, we know that, in a word like "energy," the stress placed on the first syllable is stronger than the stress on the second and third. We may also recognize, when we pronounce the word "anniversary," that the syllable with the strongest stress is the third, that the next-to-strongest stress falls on the first syllable, and that the stress placed on the remaining syllables is even less strong. From this example, we would have to conclude that spoken English admits not just two but three levels of stress. Actually, most linguists think that there are *four* levels of stress available in spoken English. If we have sensitive ears, we can probably hear that the syllable "-ry" in "anniversary" receives slightly more stress than either the syllable "-ni" (second syllable) or "-sa" (in the fourth syllable), so that, counting up, we find there are indeed four levels of stress. Although this is a fact significant in linguistics and in the refined sense of rhythm of some poets, for most metrical purposes we need consider only three levels of relative stress, which we can term "stronger," "intermediate," and "weaker." Notice that I don't label stresses as "strong" and "weak," but instead, "stronger" and "weaker." That way, we maintain the principle of *relative* stress on which meter in English is based.

There are also four *sources* of stress in English. The first is what might be called *etymological stress,* based on the word accent as found in the dictionary. If you look up the word "remake" (the verb), most dictionaries will divide the word into two syllables and place a strong mark on the second: *re-'make.* Or, with the word "remake" (the noun), the same division but a strong accent on the first syllable: *'re-make.* This kind of stress is inseparable from the identity of the word, the sonic properties that allow us to recognize it.

The second source of stress is *syntactic,* based on the importance given a word in a sentence. For example, in the sentence "Their eyes will blink," each word is monosyllabic, and each receives some stress in order to be audible; but "eyes" and "blink" receive relatively more stress than the other two words because of their syntactic importance, their crucial significance in the meaning of the statement. "Their" and "will" are understood, consciously or unconsciously, as helping words only, and so receive lighter stress.

The third kind of stress is *rhetorical* or *emphatic stress,* the vocal energy used to underline the importance of certain words in a sentence that otherwise would receive weaker stress. In the sentence "Oh, yes you *are,*" "are" is printed in italics to show that rhetorical emphasis is being added to syntactic stress the syllable would normally receive. As such, the sentence is a good reply to statements like, "I'm afraid I'm not very bright," or "No, I'm not going to aerobics class today." Emphatic stress is actually indispensable to make distinctions in the meaning of certain statements clear. Compare the sentence, "She is *my* friend," with "She *is* my friend."

The fourth kind of stress is a purely *literary* one, the stress provided by meter in lines of poetry. In ordinary conversational speech, we would hear only four stresses in the sentence, "I heard the reason for the shape it took"—i.e., the stress falling on the syllables "heard," "rea-," "shape," and "took." If this were a line of poetry, however, experienced readers of metrical verse would attribute a stress to the word "for." Doing so isn't purely arbitrary, because some careful speakers would, even without metrical prompting, place a bit more stress on "for" than on "-son" or "the." This differential is unimportant in conversation but significant for meter, in which a purely conventional stress is assigned to some syllables. Following that convention, we will place more stress on the syllable "for," promoting it, so to speak, to the intermediate level of stress somewhere between the weaker level (as in the syllables "-on" and "the") and the stronger level in the syllables "heard," "rea-," "shape," and "took."

Don't imagine that lines like the above constitute a rare case. In fact, metrically conferred accentuation is a common feature of standard prosodic practice, and sensitivity to it is a necessary part of a refined sense of poetic rhythm. Two more examples:

I seek with garlands to redress that wrong:

MARVELL, "The Coronet"

The preposition "to" receives a purely metrical stress, not as strong as "seek" but stronger than "re-."

> And, by the incantation of this verse,
>
> SHELLEY, "Ode to the West Wind"

In this line, "of" receives a metrical stress stronger than "the," though weaker than "-ta-" or "verse." In no way should the inclusion of stress conferred purely by meter be considered a compositional failing. In the best examples, the slight (incantatory?) departure from ordinary speech patterns afforded by metrical stress makes for a useful rhythmic reinforcement of the content, as we will see in a later chapter, when we discuss metrical variation.

Just to gain some perspective on the nature of English meter, we can pause for a moment to consider a few other language traditions and meters based on different auditory features of *those* languages. Recalling that *meter* means "measure," and that *measure* involves counting, what are the auditory features in any given line that might be counted? Well, the first thing that could be counted is the number of words; but since words are of variable length and accentuation, the number of words per line has never been used as the basis for meter in any language. The next feature that could be counted is the number of syllables, and this feature *has* been used as the basis for meter in several Asian languages as well as for French poetry. Why? Because Chinese, Japanese, and French lack a strong stress differential in the pronunciation of their syllables. What poets writing in these languages count instead is the number of syllables, which is always the same for each line in a poem, or, if it varies, varies according to a preset pattern. To hear the auditory effects characteristic of meter based on syllable count, try to pronounce the two lines following without making any syllable more prominent than any other, either by length or stress:

> do re me fa la
> la so mi fa do.

Each line contains the same number of syllables, and for readers in the above-mentioned languages, this quantified aspect of the lines, quite apart from syllable length or stress, is enough to register on the ear as metered poetry.

Looking at an individual line, another auditory feature that could be quantified is the number (and placement) of long syllables, at least in those languages where syllable length is particularly noticeable. Sanksrit, Greek, and Latin poetry all used syllable length in forming their meters, and the codified result is termed *quantitative meter* since it is based on "quantity," i.e., duration of syllables. Efforts have also been made in English to write using quantitative meter, but quantity has never become a widely used metrical resource in our language. Syllables in spoken English do in fact vary as to length—we need only to compare the word "smooth" with the article "a" to recognize the fact. As readers of poetry in English, though, we are conditioned to pay more attention to stress than length and for that reason fail to notice meter based on length alone. When directed to listen for this auditory feature, we can, however, hear it. To give yourself some idea how quantitative meter sounds, read the following line and, without putting stress differentials on the syllables, sustain the *oom* syllables longer than the *pa* syllable:

Oooom pa oooom pa oooom pa pa oooom pa ooom pa.

This quantitative pattern is used in the lyrics of the Greek poet Sappho. In the early classical tradition, the sense of syllable length received further reinforcement from the music that always accompanied any performance of Greek poetry because quantified duration is a primary feature of music composition.

The Teutonic languages with strong stress differentials (including German and Anglo-Saxon) developed metric systems based on the aspects of stress apart from syllable length, which is not quantified in them. Even though the number of syllables in a given line varies and syllables in the line are of differing length, Germanic and Anglo-Saxon meters rely only on the *stress* given to certain of those syllables. A possible result is as follows, where syllable stress is indicated by uppercase letters:

TA room room Ta   room TA room room TA
room TA room TA   TA room room TA room

Notice that the line is divided into two halves, with two strong stresses in each half. The stresses fall in different places, and stressed syllables are shorter than unstressed, but no matter: these lines follow the requirements for the Germanic system of *accentual meter*, which was the forerunner of our own system.

When modern English meter was being developed in the sixteenth century, poets came to use both the number of strong stress differentials *and* the number of syllables in a line to devise their meter. This is the metric scheme that has prevailed in English-language poetry right up into the contemporary period, the kind that is termed *accentual-syllabic meter* or *foot verse*. Length of the syllables is not a metric determinant, only the alternation of stronger and weaker stresses *and* the maintenance of a regular syllable count. In the following couplet (from Shakespeare's Sonnet 83), each line has five stronger stresses (and five weaker) to produce a line with ten syllables:

> There lives more life in one of your fair eyes
> Than both your poets can in praise devise.

If the rhythmic character of these lines sounds familiar, that is because Shakespeare is using the system that has formed almost all of the poetry you have ever heard or read in English.

Before looking at accentual-syllabic meter in detail, let's go back to the Teutonic system, which was the first metric system practiced by Anglo-Saxon poets writing in England in the early Middle Ages. In the accentual system, each line contains no more and no less than four strong stresses or accents; and the line is divided into two parts by a brief pause known as a *caesura* (from Latin *caedere*, "to cut"). On either side of the caesura two stresses are found. Another feature, incidentally, of Anglo-Saxon verse is the presence of *alliteration,* the use of identical initial consonants or vowels in the stressed syllables. At least one stressed syllable in the second half of a line in Anglo-Saxon verse will begin with the same consonant or vowel as a stressed syllable in the first half. All *four* stressed syllables may be alliterated, or only three, but certainly at least two, falling on either side of the caesura. Consider these lines:

> Walking west   I longed for a wellspring.
> As high as the hawk flies   the heavens were hazy.
> In that wild kingdom   nowhere was comfort
> Yet all the apples   I ate were awesome.

The space at center line marks the caesura. On either side of it, in each line you find two strong stresses. In line one, on "Walk-" and "west," and "longed" and "well-." In line two, on "high" and "hawk," and "heav-" and "ha-." In line three, on "wild" and "king-," and "no" and "com-." In line four, on "all" and "ap-," and "ate" and "awe-." The number of syllables in each line, or on either side of the caesura, varies widely: as few as three or as many as six. The meter does not take the number of syllables into account, only the number of stresses. Notice, however, that at least two of the stressed syllables in each line begin with the same consonant or vowel, as, for example, lines three and four. Note, however, that in line four it is the vowel "awe-" that is the same sound as the vowel in the monosyllable "all." That is not the same vowel sound of letter "a-" in either "apple" or "ate," and alliteration is concerned only with sound, not with spelling. Still, the requirement is that only two of the stressed syllables have to be alliterated, and, since the "a-" of "all" and the "awe-" of "awesome" are the same sound, requirements are met in this line. In line two, all four of the stressed syllables begin with the same consonant, and in line one, three of the stressed syllables do so.

Rules for Anglo-Saxon meter are almost never applied to poems written after the Middle Ages, but Anglo-Saxon poetry did influence the special rhythms and alliterative abundance characteristic of Gerard Manley Hopkins's poetic experiments. And occasionally you find a few contemporary poems that follow Anglo-Saxon rules of stress and alliteration exactly: one is Auden's "Prologue at Sixty" and another is by Richard Wilbur, titled "Junk." The Anglo-Saxon system produces verse that falls a bit strangely on contemporary ears, but that very peculiarity can be used as an expressive resource.

Meanwhile, accentual verse *without* alliteration, using more or fewer accents than the four required in Anglo-Saxon, has appeared many times in poetry since the Romantic period. The first important example is Coleridge's *Christabel,* and there have been many others since, including Auden's "Epithalamium." You often read analyses of contemporary poems where critics speak of a "three-beat" or "four-beat" line. This loose terminology (drawn from music's technical analogy) will do for poems in which the poet has counted only the stresses and not the number of syllables, allowing stresses to fall in no recurrent pattern. But in cases where the poet has used rules for accentual-syllabic verse without entire strictness, a more precise terminology is needed, and the critic should provide it.

The main problem with using stress alone as a basis for meter is that there is too much room for disagreement about which syllables actually *receive* stress. If we look at a few lines presumably written in accentual meter without alliteration, the problem becomes readily apparent. I have changed the following citation by putting all stressed syllables in uppercase:

> And the ROUGH FUture
> Of an inTRANsiGEANT
> And the beTRAYing SMILE,
> BeTRAYing, but a SMILE:
> That that is NOT, is NOT;
> ForGET, forGET.
>
> AUDEN, "His Excellency"

Nearly everyone would agree that the syllables notated here in uppercase all receive stress, and we see that there are two of these per line. Meanwhile, the syllable count is as few as four and as many as six, with stresses falling in several different places: therefore this is accentual verse. Yet some readers might also hear as stressed the syllables "And" in the first line, "Of" in the second line, and the initial "That" in the fifth line. Some readers, on the other hand, might *not* hear much stress on the syllable "-geant" in "intransigeant." Accentual-*syllabic* meter (as opposed to purely accentual meter) would certainly place stress on these syllables. Because that is the system ears conditioned by post–Anglo-Saxon practice respond to, most of us would hear those syllables with intermediate stress as part of the metrical pattern. Anyone writing in accentual meter has to overcome our expectations based on the later system—an extra compositional problem requiring laborious metrical safeguards that tend to blight spontaneity.

In Anglo-Saxon verse composition, consistent alliteration and the two-stress/caesura/two-stress system of composing a line left almost no doubt as to where the accents fell. What's more, in the early medieval period, only a few people could read at all, let alone puzzle out a meter. In practice, that meant the largest audience was composed of those who heard poems in public performance, where the author or reciter could guarantee correct accentuation of the text. In most cases, those poets also had the added support of musical accompaniment to mark the stresses. Modern readers faced with a printed page have no such assistance, unless the poet happens to have recorded the poem in question and the recording is generally available. So long as the printed page is the main avenue from poet to reader, means of establishing accentuation other than audio reproduction will be indispensable. It would be safer for poets using accentual meter to mark the stronger stresses and not leave us in doubt as to where they fall. (Granted, such visual markers are a distraction as we read a poem; but perhaps they could be indicated in a footnote.) When it comes to accentual-syllabic prosody, though, we can do without extra visual indicators because this system is able to tell us where stronger stresses fall without leaving us in much doubt; nor does it require alliteration to confirm the location of stressed syllables. (Alliteration is, in fact, still sometimes used in contemporary poetry, but more as a reinforcement of content or heightening of rhythm than for purely metrical purposes.)

Now that we have had a brief survey of other metrical systems, we should turn to accentual-syllabic prosody, which from the sixteenth through the nineteenth century governed the meter for most poetry written in English. It may come as news to some students that this system still informs a reckonable percentage of poems written in the contemporary period.

2. Accentual-Syllabic Verse

The metrical system used in most verse written in English since the sixteenth century is one called *accentual-syllabic verse,* in which stresses as well as the number of syllables per line are counted. Other names sometimes used for it are *syllable-stress verse* and *foot verse.* In this system of meter the poetic line is divided into a given number of units called *feet* (a direct translation from the Latin *pes* or the Greek *pous,* both meaning "foot" and said to refer to the foot-tapping that often accompanies strong rhythmic accents). Foot-tapping as an audience relation to music "with a beat" is common enough, but almost nonexistent when poetry is read. Greek poetry, though, was always set to music and sometimes accompanied dancing, so that the metrical foot and rhythmic patterns of the dance were closely related. In classical poetry each line was composed of a prescribed series of feet *different* in kind. In English poetry since the Renaissance, a principle of uniformity is the norm, with each foot the same (at least in principle) as all the other feet in the line. In both systems each foot has a special name and takes its identity from the fixed pattern of weaker and stronger stresses on the syllables in that foot.

The English system uses a vocabulary drawn from Greek and Latin practice, even though classical meters used length instead of stress as the basis for their meters. The most common foot in English is the *iamb* (adjectival form, *iambic*), which comes from the

Greek *iambos,* itself derived from a verb meaning "to assail." Greek verse in iambic trimeter was typically used for satiric poems, but iambic poetry in English isn't restricted to this mode—in fact, as our poetic practice has developed, iambic meter is the most "serious" that we have in English. An iambic foot consists of two syllables in sequence, a weak stress on the first syllable, followed by a strong stress on the second. If you hear syllables in the recurrent pattern "weak-STRONG, weak-STRONG, weak-STRONG," you are hearing a series of iambic feet.

We need, though, to recall that meter is based on *comparative* differences, that is, weaker stresses contrasted with stronger ones. Therefore, a more accurate description of the iambic foot is *two syllables in sequence, the second syllable receiving more stress than the first.* Let's move to actual examples. The stresses in the word "indebt" (the weaker "in-" directly followed by the stronger "-debt") correspond to those in an iambic foot. Easy enough. But the phrase "debt free" *also* constitutes an iambic foot. Why? Because, even though we do hear some stress on the word "debt," the stress on the word "free" is even stronger. Two consecutive syllables that at first glance might seem to bear equal stress turn out not to do so, on closer inspection—in this case and in most others as well. English speech habits, overall, place more stress on the *second* of two consecutive monosyllabic words, even when the first of the two has a certain amount of vocal weight. In the phrase "debt free," both syllables have roughly the same duration or length, but "free" is spoken slightly louder and at a slightly higher pitch; this vocal differential is enough to be perceived as a stronger stress, one adequate for the formation of an iambic foot.

If we look at the line

In order that the country be debt free

we can see that in conversational speech, the strongest stress would fall on the syllables "or-," "coun-," and "free," with nearly as much on the syllable "debt." Read as a line of iambic verse, though, accents would fall as follows:

In ORder THAT the COUN-try BE debt FREE.

Writing the fourth syllable "that" in all capital letters obscures the fact that it receives less stress than "or-" or "coun-"; the syllable actually receives stress at an intermediate level between the weaker and stronger stresses placed, respectively, on "In" and "or-." But we are already familiar with this special instance of metrically conferred stress, which promotes "that" to its intermediate level in order to produce an unbroken series of iambs; and we only need to consider one other factor before going on to examine a more accurate system of metrical notation than the blunt use of capital letters. If the phrase "In order that the country be debt free" is part of a metrical composition, we can disregard the purely sonic fact that, in conversational speech, the syllable "debt" receives more stress than the syllable "that." In its own foot, the last position in the line, "debt" is not as strongly stressed as "free," and so the two syllables together make up an iambic foot. In determining the nature of a foot, we consider only the relative difference between stresses in *that single foot;* it isn't necessary to compare the stress level of syllables in the foot with stress levels in other feet of the line.

The process of ranking stresses in given lines and the notation of those stresses is called *scansion* and the verb for making this notation is *to scan*. A writer of metered poetry must learn scansion in order to compose metrically, and a reader of that poetry must be able to scan its lines in order to follow the author's metrical pattern.

Several systems of notation have been used in literary history to mark the scansion of metered lines. The earliest was based on the Greek and Latin system, where the mark ∪ was placed over short syllables. Over long syllables the mark — was placed. The appearance of the two symbols suggests a difference in duration: one is visibly longer than the other, and syllable length was, in fact, the basis for classical meters. But length is not the basis for English meter, and so another mark was developed for English scansion. The symbol / was placed over syllables receiving stronger stress and the classical ∪ retained for weaker stresses. It is usual also in scansion to divide the line into its component feet by a series of vertical marks. Since a line of any length will contain somewhere in it a brief pause, analysts of meter always mark this pause, which is called—remember?—the *caesura,* with *double* vertical lines. So, for example, the marked scansion for the above line would go as follows:

In or| der that|| the coun| try be| debt free

The same system of scansion would be used for every line of the poem.

Not all metrical scholars have been content with this system of scanning verse. Some have wanted to mark three or even four levels of stress within a line. The system most commonly adopted to mark three of those levels introduces the symbol \ for intermediate stress between weak and strong. For example, in Dickinson's line

$$\cup \quad / \quad \cup / \quad \cup \quad \backslash \quad \cup \quad /$$

The Brain-|| is wi| der than| the Sky–

notice that "than" is correctly marked with this symbol, which indicates that this syllable receives less stress than the second, fourth, or eighth syllables of the line, but more than the first, third, fifth, or seventh. Note, however, that the foot "-der than" is just as much an iamb as any other foot in the line, according to metrical rules: if the second of two syllables in a foot receives stronger stress than the first, the foot is an iamb, even when the stress differential is quite small. That is true even though the line, if it were pronounced as in ordinary speech, would contain only three strong stresses, those marked with the symbol /. Given that the conventions of meter have been upheld, why take the trouble to mark an intermediate stress at all? Actually, not all metrical scholars will bother with it. Those who want to point out the difference see this small variation of stress as a rhythmic feature contributing to the sonic richness of the poem, often with an expressive justification. They assume that it is an instance of conscious aesthetic choice, one that adds to the experience and meaning of a poem. Moreover, anyone reciting the poem aloud should avoid the mistake of giving all the stresses the same force; to do so turns metered poetry into singsong. Children reciting nursery rhymes are apt to perform them as singsong by failing to distinguish among strong and intermediate stress, but adults should not imitate them. Stresses at the intermediate level must be given less strength than those at the highest level—just as they must have more weight than those at the lowest level—in order to register the line's metrical character. Marking intermediate stresses helps us perform lines of poetry as they were meant to be heard: verbal compositions with a sound system not identical to conversational habits and yet not utterly removed from them.

We can also regard the question of intermediate stress as having a relevance wider than the practical question of proper recitation. Intermediate stress is one of the markers of the relationship between conscious art and pure spontaneity. If poems were written at will, with no forethought and no revision, they would almost certainly exhibit no recurrent pattern of stresses that could be described as metrical. They would have the virtue—a real one—of spontaneity, but they would lack special pleasures that control and conscious art bring to poetry. On the other hand, if poems were written entirely according to rational prescriptions, revised only in the interest of conformity to artistic conventions, they might achieve a perfect embodiment of those conventions, including metrical norms, but they would then lack spontaneity: they would have little resemblance to common speech and would seem predictable, leaden, lifeless. What many metrical theorists try to locate is the *tension* between spontaneous utterance and speech that is aware of metrical convention. The use of intermediate stress is an index of that tension, suggesting that the poet was aware that a line of verse had speechly qualities even as it remained within indispensable metrical requirements. And in the very best instances, intermediate stress also reinforces the cognitive content of the line, as we will see in a later chapter on metrical variation.

I mentioned in the first chapter that linguists locate not three, but *four* levels of stress in English. Some metrical theorists want to mark all four of these levels when they scan. In order to do that, the following marks have been devised, moving left to right from weakest to strongest stress:

∪ \ ∧ /

These are a little confusing to the eye, and so other theorists have simply preferred to use numbers, marking the weakest with numeral 0 and so on up to 3. This suggests, though, that some syllables receive no stress at all (an impossibility), so it would seem more logical to mark stresses with numerals 1 to 4. Using this system we could scan the following line this way:

<pre>
    1   2   1 4   1 3   1 4   1 2
    We had| | a hap| py an| ni ver| sa ry.
</pre>

There is room for disagreement here, though, given that particular readers or performers of the line may stress different syllables according to different expressive impulses: some might, for example, mark the syllable "had" as a 3-level stress. Scanning all four levels of stress will, alas, lead to nearly unresolvable disputes. If, on the other hand, the two intermediate levels of stress (levels 2 and 3, the hardest to distinguish) are combined into one, we could base the scansional system on three stress levels only: weaker, intermediate, and stronger. In numerical terms, we could then mark the levels 1, 2, and 3, in the order of increasing stress. Under this system, we are much more likely to reach a consensus as to the correct scansion of any given line. In the three-level system, the above line becomes:

```
I   2    I  3    I  2    I  3    I 2
```
We had| | a hap| py an| ni ver| sa ry.

For the purposes of most discussions, this metrical notation suf-
fices. In the following pages, when an individual foot is being
marked for scansion, I will use the symbols ∪ and /. When a
whole line is being scanned and relative stress values noted, I will
use numerals 1 to 3 for stress levels from weakest to strongest.
Those readers who want to distinguish all four levels of stress may
simply divide level 2 into weaker and stronger stresses (2a and 2b)
and mark their scansions accordingly.

There are several other feet apart from iambic possible in English
verse. After iambic, the most commonly found foot is the *trochee*
(adjectival form, *trochaic,* from Latin *trochaicus,* ultimately from
a Greek verb meaning "to run"). A *trochee* is a two-syllabled foot
composed of a stronger stress followed by a weaker: / ∪. Since
both iambic and trochaic feet have two syllables, they are referred
to collectively as *duple meter.* Here is the scansion of a line of verse
with trochaic meter:

```
2  I    3     I   3  I    3  I
```
On the| shores| | of | Gitche| Gumee,

LONGFELLOW, *The Song of Hiawatha*

Note that intermediate stresses are found in trochaic meter also,
marked here by numeral 2. This is a good place to observe that
the caesura sometimes falls in the middle of a foot as it does here,

between "shores" and "of," which compose the second foot of the line. Since the caesura is a durational marking, not a stress marking, it does not interfere with the metrical scansion of the line, which is based on stress.

In English we also have *triple meter,* based on feet with three syllables. First there is the *anapest* (adjectival form, *anapestic,* from Latin *anapæstus,* ultimately from a Greek verb meaning "to strike"), which is composed of two weaker syllables followed by a stronger: ∪ ∪/. Here is a line of scanned anapestic meter:

    1   1   3   1 1   3   1   1   3   1 1   3
    And the top| of the stee| ple|| was tall| er than tall

Notice again that the caesura in this line falls in the middle of a foot, after "-ple" in the third foot of the line.

The other triple meter in English is *dactylic* (from Latin *dacty-los,* the same as the Greek word for "finger," because our fingers have three joints). A dactylic foot is composed of a stronger stress followed by two weaker stresses: / ∪ ∪. Since it corresponds to the stress pattern of ¾ time in music, it is sometimes called the *waltz-time* meter. Here is a scanned example:

    3 1 1   3 1   1 3 1 1 3   1 2
    Fanciful| ribbons|| were| given to| Catherine.

Notice that the caesura falls after "ribbons" in the middle of the second foot. Notice also that the syllable "-ine" receives intermediate stress, but the foot remains a dactyl because the stress falling on "Cath-" is still stronger.

There are two other duple feet possible but uncommon in English. The first is the *spondee* (adjectival form *spondaic,* from Latin *spondeus,* from a Greek word meaning "a solemn drink offering," associated with a kind of verse composed for such an occasion). A spondaic foot is composed of two strong stresses: / /. In practice, spondaic feet are hard to achieve in English because the linguistic tendency is always to put more stress on the second of two otherwise equal syllables, though we can come up with a few words like "archfiend" and "ice cream" or proper names like "Purcell" (as the British pronounce it) that stress both syllables about equally. In verse, punctuation is generally required to guarantee spondaic meter as in Milton's famous

> Rocks, caves,| lakes, fens,| bogs, dens| | and shades| of death,

where the first three feet may be scanned as spondees because each monosyllabic word is separated from those around it by a comma. Yet even here some metrists would mark the feet as iambs on the principle of comparative stress differences, giving more stress to "caves," "fens," and "dens" than to "Rocks," "lakes," and "bogs."

The other remaining duple meter is the *pyrrhic* (adjective and noun the same spelling, derived from Latin *pyrrhicius,* from a Greek word pertaining to a war dance). A pyrrhic foot is composed of two syllables of weak stress: ∪ ∪. Again, pyrrhics are hard to find in English because normal stress habits tend to accent one of the syllables more strongly than the other. For this reason, it isn't possible to have an entire line written in pyrrhic feet: a differential is always established among a run of more than three syllables, which means that metrical conventions have to apply and must be marked as such. The pyrrhic occasionally appears in a single foot, but then it is always followed directly by a spondee, as in this line from Pope's *The Rape of the Lock*:

```
    1    1      3        3      1   3      1 3    1      3
And the| press'd watch| | returned| a sil| ver sound.
```

It's as though the four consecutive syllables parcel out the same amount of stress as found in two consecutive iambs, but then rearrange the order of the stresses. For that reason, some theorists call this fixed pattern a *double iamb*, or even an *ionic foot*, counting it nevertheless as the equivalent of two feet, so that the regulation number of feet per line may be maintained. It may seem that we're spending too much time on a rare anomaly, but in fact the pyrrhic-spondee pattern occurs very often in English poetry. Metrists will not always agree, though, about the proper scansion of this particular rhythm. W.C. Bryant's line

```
   1    1     3   3      1   3      1   2    1   3
Where thy| pale form| was laid|, with ma| ny tears,
```

can be scanned with a pyrrhic first foot and a spondaic second foot; but some theorists would hear the first two feet as iambs, composed of increasing stress levels from 1 to 2a to 2b to 3. The comparative principle is preserved in this scansion, but the question is whether a performance close enough to normal speech patterns can be maintained when the lines are said this way:

```
   1   2a    2b    3      1   3      1   2b    1   3
Where thy| pale form| | was laid,| with ma| ny tears,
```

Still, we occasionally come across a line that does require such distinctions in order to support its content. For example, in Yvor Winters's "Time and the Garden," the line, "The future gathers in vine, bush, and tree," seems to require a four-level scansion, which makes the line iambic throughout, rather than a three-level scansion with pyrrhic and spondee.

The line scanned with three levels:

1   3   1   3   1   1   3   3   1   3

The fu| ture ga| thers| | in| vine, bush,| and tree:

The line scanned with four levels:

1   3   1   3   1   2a   2b   3   1   3

The fu| ture ga| thers| | in| vine, bush,| and tree:

The latter seems preferable (assuming the reader actually can make audible all four distinct levels) because the steadily increasing stress in the iambs of the third and fourth foot serves as a sonic reinforcement of the gradually mounting manifestations of vegetative force. The future gathers; volume augments in a steady progression. Meter marks the difference.

The poet has to determine not only what kind of metrical foot to use but also how many feet per line. The meters used most often in English are those having from three to five feet per line, but examples of shorter or longer meters can be found, with one foot the minimum, obviously, (cf. Herrick's "Upon His Departure Hence") and eight apparently the upper extreme (cf. Tennyson's

"Locksley Hall"). There are terms to describe these numbers, moving from lines of one foot to lines of eight: monometer, dimeter, trimeter, tetrameter, pentameter, hexameter (sometimes called the *alexandrine* from the French *alexandrin*), heptameter, and octameter. The description of a poem's meter must include the name of the foot followed by the term for the number of feet per line. For example, Pope's line "I lisp'd in numbers, for the numbers came" is properly described as *iambic pentameter,* five iambs composing the line. ("Numbers" is an old term for meters or verse.) And Tennyson's line (from "The Charge of the Light Brigade") "Cannon to the right of them" is described as *dactylic dimeter* because it contains two dactylic feet.

A few more examples:

> I trust we share a common dream
> As though we were a seasoned team.
>
> (IAMBIC TETRAMETER)

> And the forests they roamed in the dark
> Were less traveled than paths in the park.
>
> (ANAPESTIC TRIMETER)

> Never make an enemy of Nature;
> Never harm a beast or trusting creature.
>
> (TROCHAIC PENTAMETER)

There are many exceptions to the rule, but in general we can say that serious subjects use longer meters like pentameter and hexameter, and lighter subjects use shorter meters like trimeter and tetrameter because the shorter lines move more rapidly than the longer. Speed goes with lightness and slowness with gravity.

In most cases the number of feet per line is uniform throughout the poem, just as the kind of metrical foot is. Some verseforms (like the ballad), however, prescribe different foot numbers for some of the lines in the stanza; the *stanza* then remains uniform throughout the poem, even though some lines are longer than others within that stanza. In chapter 6 we will look at verseforms based on special stanzas. Finally, there are some poems (not always divided into stanzas) with most of the lines having a uniform number of feet, which, even so, occasionally introduce a longer or shorter line. Milton's "Lycidas," for example, is written for the most part in iambic pentameter, but nevertheless includes several lines in iambic trimeter. Not many poems use this technique, but it is effective in that one.

Meter is a guide, not a straitjacket. In principle, all the feet of lines written in any given meter are the same kind of foot. In practice, it is permissible and even *desirable* to make occasional substitutes for the governing meter in a given line, so that, for example, an iambic pentameter line commonly includes one trochaic or anapestic foot in place of one of the iambs; and sometimes it includes as many as *two* non-iambic feet. The general rule is that the substituted feet in a line will never outnumber feet of the reigning meter: in iambic pentameter you may make as many as two substitutions, but not three—because then there would be more substitutes than iambs in the line. Latitude as to the frequency of substitution permitted has varied during the history of English verse. In the early sixteenth century, substitution was common; later in the century it was discouraged. The same relaxation of the rules came in the early seventeenth century, only to be tightened during the late 1600s and strictly maintained by the Augustans. During the Romantic period, perfect regularity was not required or even much attempted in poetic composition. And the arrival of modernism meant, for the most part, a discarding of traditional metrical practice altogether in favor of various kinds of loosely metered or unmetered verse. One way to view the shift from normative to modernist practice is to say that restrictions on the substitution of feet were lifted, as well as the requirement (never universally followed even in traditional prosody) that each line contain the same number of feet. This view will not cover every case, as we will see in the chapter on *free verse*. Metrical variation within traditional prosody is so frequent as to have become standard, though, and in the next chapter we will see how poets have used variants in order to introduce rhythmic variety into their lines and so increase the expressive potential of metrical rhythm.

3. Metrical Variation

Choosing to write in meter is not the same as choosing to put poetry into a lockstep march tempo. Even the Augustan age poetic practice, though quite strict, allowed for metrical substitution, and skillful poets varied their rhythms in more subtle ways not always fully discussed in treatises on meter. Why have poets allowed for and even sought out variations in their meters? Partly to avoid the kind of boredom that inevitably arises when a stimulus is repeated over and over again. Think of hearing the same five-note tune six hundred times in succession: it's the kind of "water torture" that drives people mad. Introducing small changes in the prevailing meter is a way of giving variety to the governing sound-pattern of a poem. It also permits the poet to stay closer to the accentual patterns of spontaneous speech, thereby making a poem seem fresher, less bound by artifice. Metrical variation is of course an artistic effect, but it belongs to the category of "art that conceals art," art that revises away obvious artifice until a natural-seeming effect is achieved. Furthermore, in the hands of a skilled metrist, variation can serve as an extra expressive resource, shaping a line's rhythm so it will support the conceptual content of that line.

It's true that some critics and poets have discouraged the use of metrical variation for expressive purposes—Samuel Johnson, for example, and, in contemporary American poetry, Donald Justice.

This is the minority view, though, and any comprehensive reading of the English and American tradition of metered poetry shows that poets have almost in every case introduced variations that gave metrical support to statements being made. Faced with the task of avoiding rhythmic monotony, they make a virtue of necessity by using variation as one of the essential resources in the toolbox of craft. Pope's way of putting it in *An Essay on Criticism* is:

> 'Tis not enough no harshness gives offence,
> The sound must seem an Echo to the sense.

By "sound" Pope intends more than metrical variation alone: he means rhythm, but also rhyme and the play of consonants and vowels, as well. Metrical variation is one of the basic expressive elements in his poetry, as we saw in the line quoted in the last chapter:

> 1   1   3   3   1 3   1 3 1   3
> And the| pressed watch| | returned| a sil| ver sound.

The opening pyrrhic-spondee combination is a sonic reinforcement of the action described, in which a character in the elegant society Pope depicts in *The Rape of the Lock* pauses to check the time by pressing a watch stem so that a small interior chime will strike the closest hour. Consecutive stronger stresses in the spondaic foot "pressed watch" make a neat analogue for the action of pressing the watch, these followed by three perfect iambs whose stresses may be understood as corresponding to the sounding chimes. This is a highly specialized example of a very wide range of possible variations, each with its expressive potential. Let's look at a few more, beginning with the simplest.

The most common variation is metrical substitution, where one foot (or more) of the governing metrical foot is replaced by a foot (or feet) of another kind of meter. In iambic meter, substituting a trochee for one of the iambs is the most common variation; and it occurs most often in the first position of the line, as in Shakespeare's Sonnet 29:

2   1   1   3   1   3   1   3   1 3   1

Like to| the lark| | at break| of day| arising

where the trochaic first foot gives an energetic snap to the line (reinforced as well by the shared *l*'s and *k*'s "like" and "lark") appropriate for the early morning upward soar of Shakespeare's emblematic bird. How do our ears respond when this substitution is made? For one thing, we hear a strong stress in the first syllable where the meter makes us expect a weak stress only. This surprise gives the line a strong inaugurating rhythm that focuses special attention on the opening words—an attention justified by the sense contained in the line. Notice also that putting a trochee before an iamb also results in two consecutive syllables with weaker stress—here, "to" and "the"—a rhythm that cannot occur in a regularly iambic line. This has a speeding-up effect, adding a kind of skipping rhythm to the line, which, in this case, vividly corresponds to the darting flight of the bird.

Trochees may also come in later positions than the first foot of a line. When this happens, not only do we hear the quick skip of consecutive weakly stressed syllables, we also hear, just before them, two consecutive strongly stressed syllables, as we can see in this schema of three feet—the first iambic, the second trochaic, and the third again iambic:

◡/ /◡ ◡/

which sounds like weak-STRONG STRONG-weak weak-STRONG. The juxtaposition of the two strongly stressed syllables is sometimes referred to as *clashing accents,* because the effect is very marked. For example, look at a line from Shakespeare's Sonnet 85:

2   3   1   2   1   3   3   1   1   3
While com| ments of| your praise,| | richly| compil'd,

in which a trochaic substitution has been made in the fourth foot. The result is that we hear consecutive stronger stresses on the syllables "praise" and "rich-," followed by two weaker stresses that take us quickly to the final stronger stress, "-pil'd." The variation emphasizes the wealth of praise that has been heaped or "compil'd" on the beloved.

Trochees often substitute for the second foot of an iambic pentameter line, as in this one from Milton's *Paradise Lost*:

1 3   3 1   1   3   1   3   1 3
A mind| not to| be changed| | by place| or time.

Again we hear the rhythm expressivity afforded by the STRONG-STRONG-weak-weak-STRONG sequence, which focuses special attention on the words "mind," "not," and "changed." The same thing happens when a line's third foot is a trochaic substitution, as in this line from *Hamlet*:

> 2   3   1   2   3   1   1 3   1   2
> Nay, an| swer me:| | stand and| unfold| yourself.

And here's another example (from Wyatt's "Stand Whoso List"), in which a trochee substitutes as the fourth foot in a line:

> 1   2   2   3   1   3   3   1   1   3
> For him| | death grip| peth right| hard by| the crop

The fifth foot in this line by William Morris is a trochee:

> 1   3   1 3   1   3   1   3   3   1
> With whom| Alcme| na played,| | but nought| witting.

The Life and Death of Jason, Book II

Of these variations, the last is the least common since it gives to the conclusion of a line an inconclusive sound—a "falling" rhythm that poets can nevertheless use expressively, whenever they want to avoid the resolute finality suggested by a closing strong stress. Morris does so here, where the rhythm helps imply Alcmena's ominously incomplete knowledge of her situation.

To review a little, let's glance back at our quoted examples. In Milton's line "A mind not to be changed by place or time," the emphasis placed on the word "not" by trochaic substitution adds sharpness to the line's rendering of a mind's determination to be resolute and immutable; but it also introduces a subtle irony, too, by the use of a change in meter to reinforce a portrayal of steadfastness. In the line from *Hamlet* the command to "stand and unfold" is given more force and prominence by the clashing accents of the substitution. And in the line from Wyatt, the strong rhythmic reinforcement of the two contiguous stresses "right" and "hard" helps make palpable the fierce grip of death that is the poet's subject.

It's not uncommon for lines to contain more than one substitution. The general rule, not always observed, is that irregular feet should not outnumber regular feet in a line. That means that in tetrameter or pentameter, two substitutions per line may be made, as happens in this line from Wordsworth's "London, 1802":

3   1   1   3   1 2   3 1   1 3

England| hath need| of thee:| | she is| a fen

Here the first and fourth feet are trochees in an otherwise iambic line. The force of the poet's emotion registers in these two emphatic substitutions, the second beginning with a feminine personal pronoun echoing its referent "England" in the first foot. Consider also these two lines from Marlowe's *Hero and Leander:*

3   1 1 3   2   3   3 1   1   3

For as| a hot| proud horse| | highly| disdains

1   2   1   3   1   3   1   3   1   3

To have| his head| controlled,| | but breaks| the reins...

In the first line, trochaic substitution occurs in the first and fourth foot, part of an effect that is meant to suggest a spirited mount's straining at the bit and resisting control. In fact, the phrase "breaks the reins" falls just after the caesura in the second line. A passionate will to freedom is also suggested by a series of runovers that continue after this excerpt, as well as the noticeable alliteration of the initial consonant *h*.

A common double substitution is the pyrrhic-spondee combination discussed in an earlier chapter. Just to review this combination, where a pyrrhic directly precedes a spondee in a line otherwise iambic, look at this line from Pope's *The Rape of the Lock*:

I 3   I 3   I   I   3   3   I   3
Against| the po| ets| | their| own arms| they turned.

Here a pyrrhic substitutes in the third foot, followed by a spondee directly after. This rhythmic variation makes a noticeable effect because the two quick syllables throw the following strongly stressed ones into sharp relief, with an effect of ironic superiority.

Anapests are also often substituted in iambic lines, even though they ignore (by adding an extra syllable) one of the foundations for accentual-syllabic meter—that is, the maintenance of a uniform syllable count in each line. Normally an iambic pentameter line contains ten syllables, but making an anapestic substitution raises the count to eleven. Moreover, the anapest's two weakly stressed syllables introduce a slight instability into iambic's otherwise dependable alternation of weaker and stronger stresses: they make for a skip or faltering in the rhythm. For these reasons, the substitution of triple feet in lines of duple meter was discouraged during periods of classical strictness. Such substitutions, though, became common during the Romantic era, and have remained so. In this line from Shelley's *Prometheus Unbound*,

I   3   I 3   I   I   3   I   3   I   3
The rocks| are clo| ven,| | and through| the pur| ple night

the third foot is anapestic, a metric reinforcement for the image of broken rocks, an effect further heightened by Shelley's having the caesura divide the substituted foot into two parts. Much the same instability is suggested in this line from Wyatt's "Farewell Love":

1   3   1   1 3   1   3   1   3   1   3

Me lus| teth no lon| ger| | rot| ten boughs| to climb.

Wyatt bids farewell to love as a psychological site comparable to a tree with rotten limbs, unsafe to climb. Instability is suggested both by the anapestic substitution and the caesura division falling in the middle of a foot before the word "rotten."

Dactylic substitution occurs often enough in trochaic lines since it only adds one weak syllable to the prevailing trochaic duples, but it is rare in iambic. Why? A simple reason: a dactyl coming before an iamb produces a run of three consecutive weak stresses, a linguistic incident that accentual habits in English shy away from. However, the substitution is at least possible, as in this line:

1   3   1   3   3 1 1 1 3   1 2

I heard| the prince| | making a| remark| to you.

Since the syllables "-king," "a," and "re-" are all weakly stressed and yet consecutive, we have trouble saying them, and the effect is one of pronounced instability and awkwardness. Of course, dactylic substitution for the final foot in an iambic line wouldn't produce three consecutive weak syllables, but it would sound even stranger than the comparatively rare trochaic substitution in that position:

1 3   1 3   1   3   1   3   3 1 2
I hear| the o| cean's mus| ic| | play| endlessly.

For the same reasons just enumerated, anapestic substitution in trochaic lines is rare, though still possible:

3   1   3 1   1 1   3   3   1   3   1
Mark re| ported| a reproach| | made to| Lawrence.

The third foot, "a reproach," is an anapest, which, coming after the preceding weak stress of the syllable "-ed," gives us three consecutive weak stresses, hard to pronounce metrically. If, on the other hand, such a substitution is made in the *first* foot, the problem is avoided, but the result sounds odd:

1   1   3   3   1   3 1   3 1   3 1
As the priest| told you,| | I am| not a| doctor.

A moment's thought will make it clear why making an iambic substitution in a dactylic line poses the same problem of three consecutive weak stresses, as would the substitution of a trochee in an anapestic line. We can take our hypothesis a step further: to make a dactylic substitution in the middle of an anapestic line, or an anapestic substitution in the middle of a dactylic line, approaches a kind of limit to likelihood, since in either case a run of *four* weakly stressed syllables would result. In cases like these, though, regular habits of accentuation reassert themselves, and some of the weaker syllables will then be given extra stress so that an extra foot creeps into the line.

3 1   1   3 1 1   ? 1 3   3   1 1   3 1 2
Why did the| ravishing| Mélisande| | wound you so| cruelly?

"Mélisande" (at least, as pronounced in French) is an anapest, but, inevitably, the reader will give the syllable "Mé-" an extra stress not attributed to it in other rhythmic contexts in order to avoid a run of four unstressed syllables ("-vishing Méli-"); and the pentameter becomes a hexameter.

Because of the linear nature of poetry, the beginnings and endings of a line (which demarcate it as a separate unit) are areas of greater metrical sensitivity: the opening and closing feet of a line are subject to special treatment. As we've seen in the preceding discussion, trochaic substitution is most frequent in the first foot of an iambic line and rarest in the last. Another kind of metrical variation concerns the addition of one or more weakly stressed syllables at the beginning or ending of lines. An extra, weak syllable coming at the end of a line is sometimes termed a *feminine ending,* or, more technically, *final hypercatalexis.* This metrical feature is so common in English poetry it hardly registers as a variation at all. You may not even have noticed it in the line about the lark quoted from Shakespeare's Sonnet 29 several pages back, which concludes with the foot "arising," an iamb plus an additional weakly stressed syllable. Lines using this variation are said to conclude with *falling rhythm,* or a *dying fall,* which is usually soothing, lulling, graceful, as in this couplet from one of the lyrics in Dryden's *Cleomenes*:

<pre>
 3   1   3   1   1 3   1   3   1 3 1
Time and| Death shall| depart,| | and say| in flying,
</pre>

3   1   2   3   1   3   1   3   1   3 1

Love has| found out| a way| to live,| by dying.

The addition of the extra, weak syllable at the end is not regarded as altering the nature of the last foot, which still counts as iambic.

One or more unstressed syllables are often added at the beginning of the line, a practice known as *anacrusis* or *initial hypercatalexis*. It commonly occurs when the conjunction "and" or monosyllabic prepositions or conjunctions appear as first words of the line, as here in Blake's "Piping Down the Valleys Wild":

1 1   3   1   3   1   3

So I piped| | with mer| ry chear.

The initial pair of weakly stressed syllables lends a skipping rhythm to the line, a folklike quality appropriate here to the subject. But anacrusis may also be used in graver contexts—for example, this line from Shelley's "Ode to the West Wind":

1 1   3   1   3   1   3   1   3   1   3

Of the dy| ing year,| | to which| this clo| sing night

Notice that the opening foot is indistinguishable from anapestic. Even so, we consider the foot iambic, in a line composed with anacrusis. As such, it's not a strongly marked variation, but instead an extra rhythmic detail that adds expressive variety to iambic meter. Sometimes the poet uses both anacrusis and final hypercatalexis in the same line. Consider this pentameter line from Hart Crane's "Voyages":

```
 I   I  3   I     2    I  3   I  3   I  3  I
```
And in an| swer| | to| their tre| ble in| ter jections,

Iambic pentameter normally has ten syllables per line, but here, because of both initial and final hypercatalexis (or anacrusis and the dying fall), the count is twelve. The line stays within limits of normative meter, but the variations force us to read the line with more energy and rapidity, qualities that correspond to the excited cries of the children.

I will offer some more evidence that the beginning and ending of lines receive special metrical treatment by observing that weakly stressed syllables are also often omitted from the opening foot of iambic lines, and also from the *final* foot of trochaic lines. Again, the line's normal syllable count is not maintained, but instead is reduced by one. This common metrical practice is termed *truncation* or *catalexis,* labeled *initial* at the beginning of the line and *final* at the end. Some metrists prefer to restrict the meaning of *catalexis* to final truncation only. In their system, initial truncation (which can occur only in iambic and anapestic meters) should be called *acephalexis* or *acephaly.* The adjectival form is *acephalous,* which means "headless." In order not to multiply terminology in this book, I will only use the terms *initial hypercatalexis* and *final hypercatalexis* for weakly stressed syllables added at the beginning or ending of lines, and *initial truncation* or *final truncation* for lines in which weakly stressed syllables are missing from the first or last foot.

Initial truncation is so common we almost fail to hear it as a variation at all. Only think of the child's prayer "Now I lay me down to sleep," the first line of which is iambic tetrameter with initial truncation. Meanwhile, the second line uses all regular iambic feet, without truncation: "I pray the Lord my soul to keep." Truncation is of course possible in the triple meters also. Consider these lines from Byron's "The Destruction of Sennacherib":

I   I   3   I I 3   I   I   3   I   I 3

Like the leaves| of the for| est when sum| mer is green,

I   3   I   I   3   I   I 3   I   I 3

That host| with their ban| ners|| at sun| set were seen:

Note that one of the weak stresses in the opening anapest of the second line is missing—initial truncation in anapestic meter. The effect in this meter is to make the rhythm a bit less hectic, a bit less bouncy. For modern sensibilities the trap-drum insistence of triple meter rules it out for almost all poetry except comic verse; but truncation chastens it, sometimes enough to make anapestic (or dactylic) available for poetry in a serious vein.

It is also possible for *both* weakly stressed syllables to be truncated from an anapestic foot, as they are in the line "I and my Annabel Lee," from the Poe poem of that name. "Annabel Lee" is written in alternating anapestic tetrameter and anapestic trimeter, and the line just quoted is one of the trimeters, with truncation of both weak stresses from the first foot. This comes as a welcome departure from untruncated lines like "Of my darling, my darling, my life and my bride," a regular anapestic tetrameter appearing later in the poem.

An example of final truncation in dactylic meter is found in Tennyson's "The Charge of the Light Brigade":

3   1   1   3   1   1

Cannon in| front of them

3   1   1   3   1

Volley'd and| thundered;

The first line is dactylic dimeter, and so is the second, with final truncation of one weakly stressed syllable.

When dealing with what appear to be truncations, it's important to look at the whole poem to determine the governing meter because individual lines with truncation are sometimes impossible to describe with certainty by themselves. If we consider the first line (which is used as the title) of a poem by Ben Jonson,

3   1   3   1   3   1   3

Queen and huntress, chaste and fair,

we can tell which accents are weaker and which stronger, but we can't tell from this line *by itself* whether it should be divided into four iambic feet with initial truncation, or four trochaic feet with *final* truncation. The poem follows this pattern consistently until the third stanza where the lines "And thy crystal-shining quiver" as well as "Space to breathe, how short soever" appear, both of these regular trochaic lines. They suffice to establish that the meter is trochaic throughout, with all other lines subject to final truncation. Our doubts are resolved. Note, on the other hand, that we sometimes find poems like Emerson's "Self-Reliance," written in a tetrameter following the pattern of Jonson's first line and following that pattern throughout, none of the lines anywhere in the poem beginning or ending with weakly stressed syllables. That fact makes it impossible for us to describe the meter as either iambic or trochaic.

          3   1   3   1   2   1   3
     Cast the bantling on the rocks,

          3 1   2   1   1   3   1   3
     Suckle him with the she-wolf's teat,

          3   1   2   1   3   1   3
     Wintered with the hawk and fox,

          3   1   3   1   3   1   3
     Power and speed be hands and feet.

Emerson has made a substitution in line two, the extra weakly stressed syllable "the." If the meter is iambic, then the third foot "with the she-" is anapestic. If the meter is trochaic, the second foot "him with the" is dactylic. But we can't decide which is the correct description, no more than in the case of Emerson's "The Humble-Bee," most of whose lines begin and end with a strongly stressed syllable—most, but not all. A few begin with a weakly stressed syllable and a few *end* with a weakly stressed syllable; choosing then to describe the poem as written in either iambic or trochaic would be arbitrary. Nor is the strong-weak-strong-weak-strong-weak-strong stress pattern a purely antiquated meter. A well-known contemporary example is the third section of Auden's "In Memory of W.B. Yeats," which presents the same problem of undecidability.

Poems in tetrameter following this format have been so common in English poetry and hymnody that perhaps a special name for them ought to be devised, since we can't say whether they are iambic or trochaic. Their existence has supported an argument made by some metrical theorists who regard the iambic-trochaic (as well as the anapestic-dactylic) distinction as superfluous. They would say that meter is either duple or triple, period; that, if initial and final hypercatalexis and truncation are factored in, any line can be analyzed as simply either duple or triple. But I don't see what's gained by conflating the two species of duple and triple meter, particularly since English-language poets have always kept those distinctions in mind as they composed their lines. However, when dealing with indeterminate poems in tetrameter with either initial or final truncation, perhaps we could apply the term "truncated duple tetrameter," allowing that, in this case, there is no way to apply the iambic-trochaic distinction. The same problem could, by the way, arise with the triple meters as in the following lines:

> 3   1   1 3 1   1 3   1   1 3
> Why not petition Renée and Marie,

> 3   1   1 3   1   1 3 1   1   3
> Neither a person of minor degree?

Is this anapestic tetrameter with the two weaker syllables of the first foot truncated? Or dactylic tetrameter with the final two weaker syllables truncated? Impossible to say. I'm not aware of any poems using this meter throughout, but if they exist, perhaps we could say they were written in truncated triple tetrameter.

Truncation of weaker syllables also occurs occasionally in feet other than the first or last. For example, in Wyatt's "Process of Time," we find the line

  2   3   1   3   3   1   2   1   3
Nought hel| peth tyme,| | hum| bleness,| nor place.

The third foot is missing its weaker stress. Even though the pause (marked by a comma) may be considered as replacing a weaker stress, since there is no actual syllable present, we call the third foot "truncated," and this is an example of *internal* truncation. Some theorists call feet like these *defectives,* but the term has a faintly pejorative resonance, as though the foot were somehow a mistake. An alternative term is the *monosyllabic foot,* which is considered iambic in iambic lines and trochaic in trochaic lines, even though such feet have only one syllable (always strongly stressed). Here is another example of internal truncation, this one from Marlowe's "The Passionate Shepherd to His Love":

> Come live with me and be my love,
> And we will all the pleasures prove
> That valleys, groves, hills, and fields,
> Woods, or steepy mountain yields.

The first two lines are perfectly regular iambic tetrameter; line four is regular except for initial truncation. And line three has been internally truncated to produce the monosyllabic iamb "hills." The variation offers a nice rhythmic snap to the line, as though reins were suddenly tightened or a syncopated step intervened in a regular dance.

This is a good place to expand the discussion of multiple

substitutions in a line. We've noted that irregular feet must never outnumber regular in a standard line. With that guideline in mind, how would you scan the following line if it came from a poem written in iambic pentameter?

3 1   2   1   3   1 3 1 1   3

Visions that you dreamed of rose from the earth.

At first glance, this might look like four trochees followed by a final iamb. Since the reigning meter is iambic pentameter, we know that four consecutive trochees would break the rule saying substituted feet must not outnumber standard feet. Is there a way to reconcile this? Yes, if we regard the first foot as a truncated iamb, followed by three regular iambs, with anapestic substitution in the last foot. The line then remains within necessary restrictions and is entirely acceptable. On the other hand, if the reigning meter of a poem was iambic pentameter, and the following line appeared in it,

1 3   3 1   3 1 1 3   3 1

A good| metrist|| doesn't| insult| hearing,

it's clear that the line goes outside metrical guidelines, given that the second, third, and fifth feet are trochees. When two irregular feet appear consecutively, they tend to undermine the metric standard, and the addition of one more irregular nonadjacent foot in the line definitively destroys that standard. Nevertheless, we sometimes see such lines in canonical poets, one famous example the Keats sonnet that begins with this line:

```
3   I   I   3      3   I   3   I   I   3
```
How ma| ny bards| | gild the| lapses| of time!

You might rescue this line for regularity by describing the first foot as a 2-3 iamb, which is within the realm of spoken possibility, and then call "gild" a monosyllabic foot, and the line's last three syllables an anapest, with these results:

```
2   3   I   3      3   I   3   I   I   3
```
How ma| ny bards| | ( ) gild| the lap| ses of time!

But the line remains uncomfortable, partly because of our uncertainty over its proper scansion. Maybe we can justify this odd arrangement of stresses by observing that the topic "lapses of time" is seconded by what seems to be a "lapse" in metrical proficiency; paradoxically, an awkward rhythm is just the one called for here. Poets with less mastery than Keats might want, however, to avoid doubtful lines like this one.

At the risk of overinsistence, let's go back to the truth that, in determining the governing meter, you need to consider the poem as a whole: a single line—given the factors of metrical substitution, intermediate stress, and truncation—can be scanned in more than one way. Look at the sentence, "But Red Rover had only one passion." If the preceding line (and the majority of the poem's lines) had been anapestic trimeter, as in, say, "Then my brother remembered to call," we would scan the line this way:

```
I   I   3   I   I   3   I   I   3   I
```
But Red Ro| ver had on| ly one passion.

This is anapestic trimeter with final hypercatalexis, and not especially irregular. On the other hand, if the preceding line (and the majority of the poem's lines) had been iambic pentameter, as in, say, "My brother hoped we'd all enjoy ourselves," then the line would be scanned as follows:

1 2   3 1   1 3 1 3   3 1
But Red| Rover|| had on| ly one| passion.

This is iambic pentameter, with trochaic substitutions in the second and fifth feet. Situations as ambiguous as this one rarely arise, but even the possibility thereof reminds us to be circumspect before scanning a given line. If we didn't know, for example, that Shakespeare's sonnets were all composed in iambic pentameter, we might be led to scan the opening line of Shakespeare's Sonnet 30 as follows:

3   1 1   3 1   1   3   1 1   3
When to the| sessions of| sweet silent| thought,

which would be correct if it were followed by the line, "Error abandons the truth that I sought." The sonnet is actually written in iambic pentameter, so we scan the line this way:

3   1 1 3   1 2   2 3 1   3
When to| the ses| sions of| sweet si| lent thought

and it is followed by the perfectly regular iambic line, "I summon up remembrance of things past."

The rule excluding the practice of making two *successive* metrical substitutions (one directly after another) has a notable exception.

Established metrical practice allows for two trochaic substitutions at the beginning of a line of iambic pentameter, a fact that is connected to the special status of line beginnings. An example, from Shakespeare's Sonnet 116:

$$3 \quad 1 \quad 3 \quad 1 \quad 1 \quad 3 \quad 1 \quad 2 \quad 2 \quad 3$$

Let me| not| | to| the mar| riage of| true minds

And another, from Arnold's "Dover Beach":

$$3 \quad 1 \quad 2 \quad 1 \quad 1 \quad 3 \quad 1 \quad 2 \quad 1 \quad 3$$

Heard it| on the| Aege| an,| | and| it brought

On the other hand, successive trochaic substitutions are never found at the *end* of an iambic line, or in the middle.

In principle, the governing meter of a poem is uniform throughout, but we have been looking at the phenomenon of metrical substitution as a major exception to that rule. Another qualification has to be introduced as well, this one concerning the number of feet in the poem's lines. In some cases, it isn't possible to state for the poem as a whole the number of feet per line (tetrameter or pentameter, for example) because the number varies from line to line. The first reason for the variation is that some stanzas or verseforms require differing numbers of feet for different lines in the form. The ballad, for instance, requires iambic tetrameter for the first and third lines of its individual stanzas, and iambic trimeter for the second and fourth lines. Some poets (George Herbert is especially known for doing this) have invented stanza forms

that prescribe a different number of feet for each line of the stan-
za, so that it isn't possible to give a single number-classification
of the meter. What we have to do in describing such a poem is to
say (hypothetically), "This poem is written in iambic meter, but it
is *heterometric*, with individual lines ranging from trimeter to hex-
ameter." We can go on to specify exact numbers for each line if
we're giving a detailed description. But the general term for such
poems is *heterometric*.

In some instances, there is no stanzaic pattern for the length
of lines in heterometric poems: they are longer or shorter depend-
ing on the poet's ad hoc decisions. An early example of this was
developed by John Skelton and bears the name *skeltonics*, or *tum-
bling verse*. One of the best-known examples is Skelton's "To Mis-
tress Margaret Hussey," a gaily improvised paean in a lighthearted
vein to the poet's beloved. Line lengths follow no restriction but
the poet's caprice, and the improvisatory aspect of the poem fits
the tone and subject very well. But there are other, more solemn
poems with line lengths arbitrarily varied—Milton's "Lycidas," for
example, which is written mostly in iambic pentameter yet with a
few trimeter lines appearing from time to time, in no set pattern.
The variation provides a small rhythmic lift, thereby preventing
the poem from bogging down in its stately processional.

For an even less predictable instance, look at Browning's
"Home-Thoughts from Abroad," which contains lines with as
few as two iambic feet and as many as five, appearing at what seem
to be purely spontaneous intervals. Actually, it's hard to agree on
the number of feet in some of the lines. For example, "While the
chaffinch sings on the orchard bough" might be tetrameter with

anacrusis and an anapestic substitution in the third foot. Or it might be scanned as follows:

2   1   3   1   3   1 1 3   1   3

While| the chaf| finch sings| | on the or| chard bough

in which case it is iambic pentameter, with initial truncation and an anapest substituted in the fourth foot. But is it really iambic? It might be trochaic pentameter, with the final two feet iambic substitutions. That would at least keep the rule that the governing feet in a line must be in the majority. How to decide? The usual method is to survey the whole poem, as we know. However, in the first section of the poem, most of the lines seem trochaic, and in the second section, most (but not all) seem iambic. Because there is no discernible overall regularity, the scansion of particular lines is left in doubt. We can at least say the meter is duple, but not whether it's iambic or trochaic; equally difficult to decide is the precise number of feet in some of the lines. Browning's poem, then, written in 1845, begins to move toward the irregular and metrically indeterminate line that has been dominant in free-verse practice of the twentieth century. Another such example (a sort of companion piece to the earlier and more regular "The Charge of the Light Brigade") is Tennyson's "The Charge of the Heavy Brigade." The later poem exhibits a pattern of strong and weak stresses throughout, but the pattern constantly varies, with the result that we can't with complete certainty name the meter of some of its lines.

An instance of what might be called *regularized* variation is *logo-aedic verse,* a mixture of duple and triple meter, with a prescribed or varying number of substitutions in each line. A common instance is iambic tetrameter with one anapestic substitution per line—which, for example, is mostly the rule in Robert Frost's "The Road Not Taken." Consider the following lines:

> 2   3   1   3   1 1 3   1   3
> Two roads| diverged| in a yel| low wood,

> 1   3   1 1   2   1   3   1   3
> And sor| ry I could| not tra| vel both...

In fact, with a few exceptions, all the poem's lines include an ana-pest. Three of them contain *two* anapests, and four are regular iambic tetrameter. But the variation is so consistent it has to be taken as a definite pattern. The result in this case is to give the poem a lilting, folklike quality—and also to reinforce the idea of divergent paths, for which the omnipresent iambs and anapests serve as metrical emblems. For another example of logoaedic verse, look at the chorus beginning with the line "When the hounds of spring are on winter's traces," from Swinburne's *Atalanta in Calydon.* In a poem of fifty-six lines, all but three include an anapest, and most have more than one; anapestic feet, in fact, outnumber the iambic feet in the majority of the lines. Is the meter then iambic or anapestic? Rather than attempting to decide for one or the other, we can describe the lines as *logoaedic,* and let it go at that.

This chapter is titled "Metrical Variation," but I'd like to intro-
duce a distinction here and discuss *rhythmic variation,* which is not
quite the same thing. If we look at the following (nonconsecutive)
lines from Robert Graves's "The Persian Version," we can discover
the distinction I mean:

1   3   1   3   1   3   1   3   1   3

By three| brigades| of foot| and one| of horse

1   3   1   2   1   3   12   1   3

And on| ly in| cident| ally| refute

Both lines contain five iambic feet; therefore they are metrically
identical. But they are not *rhythmically* identical because the feet
are made up of different kinds of stresses. All the stronger stresses
of the line first cited are at level 3, whereas, in the second line, the
stronger stresses of the second and fourth foot come in only at
level 2. The result is that the rhythm of the first line is much more
vigorous than in the second, more tentative one; and the distinc-
tion is well adapted to the lines' respective content.

Let's also focus on another feature: in the first line, the foot
divisions coincide with the word-ends. That is inevitable in lines
composed of monosyllabic words; in this line, all the words are
monosyllabic except "brigades," and "brigades" also happens to
compose a complete iambic foot. In the second line, though, foot
division coincides with word-end in the word "refute" only. Other-
wise the line's iambs are composed by joining weakly and strong-
ly stressed syllables from adjacent words. As subtle as this differ-
ence is, it nevertheless registers significantly on any ear prepared

to notice it. Metrical theorists have in fact noticed, and there are words from classical terminology to describe the difference: when foot divisions coincide with word-ends, the meter is said to exhibit *diaresis;* and when foot divisions do not coincide with word divisions, the meter exhibits *caesura.* Both these terms also have *other* meanings, in linguistics and meter—leading, potentially, to confusion in technical discussions. For that reason, I propose another pair of terms—*disjunctive feet* and *connective feet*—for the distinction. In lines with *disjunctive feet* (where foot divisions coincide with word-ends), words are set off from each other; they tend to be heard more distinctly as separate verbal events. By contrast, in lines with *connective feet* (where foot divisions fall between syllables of different words), words interact more cohesively; the line will sound more like a seamless unit. In Graves's poem, the line about the brigades highlights the distinction between two divisions of the army by using disjunctive feet; in the second line, a single strong word, "refute," makes up a disjunctive foot, the rest composed of connective feet, so that this one word gets special attention and emphasis.

We should, when considering rhythmic variation, pay further attention to the effect of intermediate stresses in shaping the rhythm of lines. Let's look at two more nonconsecutive lines from Graves's "The Persian Version":

$$1 \quad 3 \quad 1 \quad 3 \qquad 1 \quad 3 \quad 1 \quad 2 \quad 1 \quad 3$$

To con| quer Greece| |—they treat| it with| contempt;

$$1 \quad 3 \quad 1 \quad 3 \quad 1 \quad 2 \quad 1 \quad 3 \quad 1 \quad 3 \quad 1$$

The Per| sian mon| arch| | and| the Per| sian nation

Both lines are iambic pentameter, with no substitutions. And yet their rhythm is subtly different. Why? Because one foot in each line is formed on a 1-2 stress-level differential, rather than the 1-3 differential of the other feet. In the first line, that is the case with the fourth foot; in the second, with the third foot. Poets skilled in meter constantly play with this distinction—just as they do with the iambs formed on a 2-3 stress-level differential. Let's look at a couplet from the Graves poem:

    1   3   2   3   1   2   2   3   1 3
    (Their left| flank cov| ered| | by| some ob| solete

    2   3   1   3   1   1   3   3   1   3
    Light craft| detached| | from the| main Per| sian fleet)

The first line's second foot is a 2-3 iamb, as is the fourth foot; meanwhile the third foot is a 1-2 iamb. The passage through these iambs built on different stress levels makes for a subtle rhythmic modulation, and the momentum is continued on across the enjambment to another 2-3 iamb, "Light craft." The second line's third and fourth feet are a pyrrhic-spondee sequence, another expressive touch. Taken together, the lines of the couplet have a rhythmic freshness achievable only by unusual metrical skill—their meter's normative, certainly, and yet the rhythm is unusual.

Metrical theory has yet to devise a complete classification of the ways that poets use these stress-level distinctions, but a provocative discussion thereof is found in Nabokov's *Notes on Prosody* (see Selected Bibliography). What the serious beginning metrist should do is take note not only of the nature of the feet in a line, but of the varying stress levels composing these feet as well, and whether they are connective or disjunctive.

It may be helpful at this point to look at a few examples from recent poetry to see these metrical and rhythmic resources at work. Consider, for example, these lines from R.S. Gwynn's "Release":

2   3   2   3   1 2 1 3   1 3

Toward sun| light,| | grace| ful as| a line| of sail

3 1   1 2 1   3   3 1   1 3

Coming| into| the wind.| | Slow for| the mill-

2   3   1 3   1   2   1 3   1   3

Wheel's heft| and plum| met, | | for| the chug| and churn

1 3   1 2 1 3 1

Of wa| ter as| it gathers,

Using a measure of correct iambic pentameter, Gwynn skillfully varies the meter with a trochee ("Slow for"), to decelerate the progress of the line. Notice that the position of the caesura changes, though keeping generally to the middle of the line. Furthermore, he uses iambs not only of the 1-3 type but also some 1-2 and 2-3 iambs—a subtle modulation of the rhythm that suits the actions being described. Connective feet and disjunctive feet alternate, a seamless effect interrupted by separate chops of the millwheel. Expressive attention to consonantal sound is evident in the play of *l*'s, *t*'s, and *ch*'s, which combine to suggest grace and fluidity as well as energetic water-splashing; and we recall that "rhythm" is derived from a Greek word meaning "to flow."

Two lines from Mary Jo Salter's "The Hand of Thomas Jefferson," where she describes him holding up to the light a thermometer:

> his instrument, and read it like a vein
> pulsing with the newborn body's powers.

Looked at in isolation, the second line cited would be described as trochaic pentameter. But the poem is written throughout in iambic, so we should scan it as iambic with a truncated first foot and final hypercatalexis. We are propelled into the line by enjambment from the previous line, where initial truncation makes a strong rhythmic effect comparable to syncopation in music:

3   1   2   1 3   2   3   1   3   1
pul| sing with| the new| born bod| y's powers.

The sense of vascular pulsation is conveyed, both by the syncopation and by the steady alternation of stronger and weaker stresses. Only the foot "-sing with" is disjunctive, all the others connective, with the result that the line is strongly cohesive. It gathers vigor as it moves along, the fourth foot a 2-3 iamb with both syllables having an initial "b" consonant, concluding with the strong plosive "p" in "powers," echoing the first consonant of the line.

A line from Dana Gioia's "California Hills in August" exemplifies one of those cases in which we really need to discern four levels of stress in order to understand the meter.

> And hate the bright stillness of the noon
> without wind, without motion,

Line one above might at first look like an iambic pentameter line, with internal truncation producing a monosyllabic third foot; but lines throughout the poem are in tetrameter, so we need to find four feet here. The first iamb is "And hate"; the second foot substitutes an anapest, "the bright still-"; and the remaining feet, "-ness of" and "the noon," are iambs. Any sensitive ear will notice, however, that "bright" receives more stress than "of." Therefore the line needs to be scanned with four levels, as follows:

          1   3   1   2b   3   1   2a   1   3
          And hate| the bright still| ness of| the noon

Rhythm based on subtly contrasting stress-level is expressive here. Weight in the line accumulates in the center, with those contiguous syllables "bright" and "still-," which seem to hang suspended in a stillness like the noontime immobility of the California hills. If the word "bright" were dropped, the line would then be more regular, but nearly all its rhythmic expressiveness would vanish. The next line ("without wind, without motion") continues in the same vein, truncating the second and fourth feet, so that two stronger stresses fall together with the same sort of suspended immobility: "-out wind" and "-out mo-."

Before citing another poet, it needs to be noted that with several words in English the stress levels change according to syntactic and rhythmic context. Disyllabic prepositions like "into," "without," "within," and "inside," as well as conjunctions like "whereas," "therefore," and "wherefore," adverbs like "almost" and "henceforth," and many adjectives (including the numerals in "-teen" like "thirteen"), plus a number of words imported from French like "château" and "chauffeur" may receive stronger stress on the first *or* second syllable. Lines containing these words should be sounded carefully, with attention paid to sentence rhythm, meter, and emotional emphasis, in order to mark the stresses accurately. In her poem "My Father's Gun," Elise Paschen was able, in the compass of a single line, to use both alternative stress patterns on the word "within." We might assume at first reading that her line "a wake of rings within rings within rings" was iambic tetrameter, the third and fourth feet anapestic substitutions. But the poem is written throughout in iambic pentameter, so we are required to discover another scansion for it, and, again, four levels of stress are needed to follow the meter:

1   3   1   3   1 2   2a   2b   1   3

a wake| of rings| | within| rings with| in rings.

This scansion keeps five feet for the line. Also, the rhythmic play among four stress levels, the shift of stress pattern between the first and second "within," and the line's three alliterated *w*'s serve as a subtle sonic reinforcement for the visual image the author is describing—expanding concentric circles on a water surface. Notice that the first "within" is a disjunctive foot, while the next "within," connects two adjacent feet. Visual complexity is seconded by meter that itself takes some study and sorting out.

4. Phonic Echo

In even a short run of spontaneous, unliterary speech, some combinations of consonants and vowels are certain to recur, even though we don't take special note of them. On the other hand, if a few vowels and consonants recur with more than average frequency, we can't *avoid* noticing their sound, and we become conscious of words as an auditory experience, not merely as a medium for conveying information. For many centuries now English poetry has used this recurrence of sound expressively, organizing phonic repetition so that it becomes clearly audible and relevant to other constructive aspects of a poem. We have already seen how Anglo-Saxon poetry used *alliteration*—the repetition of words' initial consonants or vowels—as a reinforcement of accentual meter. Alliteration's potential for euphony or emphasis has also been used in poetry after the Anglo-Saxon period, as in these lines from Coleridge's *The Rime of the Ancient Mariner*:

> The fair breeze flew, the white foam flew,
> The furrow followed free.

The abundance of alliterated *f*'s registers as a phonic emblem of the ship's swift passage through wind and wave: the expulsion of air required by this fricative consonant reproduces the friction of the winds around the observing consciousness of the poem.

Alliteration is sometimes called *head rhyme,* suggesting that it is a form of rhyme in general. Alliteration and rhyme are both forms of echoed sound, but rhyme is a more complex instance of that. The word takes its origin from the same Greek and Latin words that produced the companion word "rhythm" in English, but until the seventeeth century it was spelled "rime," and reappeared with that spelling in archaizing contexts (like Coleridge's above) well into the nineteenth century. One of rhyme's functions, in fact, is to assist in establishing the rhythm or meter of a series of lines; but rhyme is not the same thing as rhythm.

Traditional or *normative rhyme,* the kind used in most poetry from the Middle English period up to twentieth-century modernism, is defined as follows: it is the duplication, at the ends of two or more lines of a given poem, of *some* of the sounds in the last strongly stressed syllable of those lines, plus duplication of *all* the sounds in any weakly stressed syllables that might follow the strongly stressed syllable. The stressed syllable, then, is the linchpin of rhyme. In normative rhyme, the vowel of the stressed syllable, and any consonant sound that might follow it, must be the same in both rhyming words. But there is one other requirement: the consonant sounds preceding the vowel of the stressed syllable should be *different* in each rhyming word. So then, if "so" and "go" come at the ends of lines in a given poem, they are normative rhymes because they are both strongly stressed syllables having the same vowels and preceded by different consonants. Likewise, if "abound" and "round" appear at line ends, they are normative rhymes because in the stressed syllables "-bound" and "round," identical vowel sounds are followed by identical consonant sounds, just as they are preceded by *different* consonant sounds. On the other hand, "relate" and "late" are not normative rhymes because, although they conform to all other requirements, the consonant preceding the stressed vowel is the same one. Finally, "lotion" and "motion" are normative rhymes because different consonants precede the vowel of the duplicated stressed syllable, which ends in "-o," and this syllable is followed by the same sound in the concluding weakly stressed syllable "-tion." Note that normative rhyme is based on *sound,* not spelling. Despite different spellings, "height" and "write" have some of the same sounds and therefore qualify as rhymes, as do "emotion" and "ocean." Stressed syllable "no" rhymes with "glow," because the consonant *w* in the second word is silent.

Keeping in mind the concept of strongly stressed syllables as the central component of normative rhyme, we can make a useful distinction by defining *double rhyme* as rhyme involving two syllables, a strongly stressed syllable followed by a weakly stressed, as in "seated" and "greeted." ("Rating" and "berating" would not qualify as normative double rhymes, though, because of the duplicate initial consonant sound in the stressed syllable.) In the same way, *triple rhyme* involves three syllables, a strongly stressed followed by two weakly stressed syllables, as "verily" and "merrily." Double rhyme, since it involves the so-called *feminine ending* or *falling rhythm,* has been used for special effects in poetry, but is often criticized as being too insistently noticeable and, as such, an aesthetic defect; nevertheless, poets continue to use it. Triple rhyme, even more insistent, has been reserved since the Romantic era almost exclusively for comic effects. This is particularly true with "mosaic" or "wrenched" rhymes, where the extra syllables are provided by more than one word, as in Byron's notorious couplet from *Don Juan*:

> But, oh! ye lords of ladies intellectual,
> Inform us truly,— have they not henpeck'd you all?

Normative rhyme has been the standard for our poetry, but many variants also exist and have become common since the nineteenth century. The most frequent departure is failing to observe the rule that consonant sounds preceding the vowel in the stressed syllable should be different, so that rhymes like "late" and "relate" appear very often, occasionally with an expressive justification. (The exclusion of such rhymes, by the way, is a convention in English poetry but not in French. In French, rhymes like "late" and "relate" are regarded as preferable to rhymes like "bait" and "relate"—or, to give French examples, *connu/nu* is regarded as more perfect that *obscur/futur*.)

Another departure from normative rhyme has to do with vowels that do not quite match. In the Sonnets, Shakespeare again and again rhymes "love" with "prove." When he wrote, however, the vowels of these two words were pronounced alike, so no infraction was involved. They no longer have the same sound, but later writers, perhaps influenced by Shakespeare's example, have sometimes rhymed them, even in the twentieth century. This kind of rhyming is known as *historical rhyme*. A related variant is what we call *eye rhyme,* the rhyming of two syllables where vowels pronounced differently are spelled the same and so used as rhyme. A well-known example is from Donne's "Go and Catch a Falling Star":

> And find
> What wind
> Serves to advance an honest mind.

"Wind" shares a spelling with the other rhyming words, but even in Donne's day its vowel was not pronounced the same as theirs. He uses this noncorrespondence to reinforce his meaning: "wind" is not an "honest" rhyme for "find" or "mind": it rhymes by cheating, so to speak, and a semantic dimension has been added to the purely conventional juxtaposition of two words with dissimilar sounds.

A special case of phonic echo is *internal rhyme*, the presence of rhyming words *within* the line rather than at the end (though end-words may also rhyme), as in this line from Hopkins's "God's Grandeur": "And all is seared with trade; bleared, smeared with toil": here, the three rhymes in "-eared" appear within the line, while "toil" rhymes with "soil" at the end of the next line. Since the phonic echo is insistently noticeable in lines like this one, internal rhyme is reserved for moments of emotional emphasis. It can add to the sonic richness of a line so long as it doesn't get out of hand and stray into artificiality. Comparable to internal rhyme is *interlinear internal rhyme* (rhyme between words not in end position), as in Shelley's "Stanzas Written in Dejection":

> Till death like sleep might steal on me,
>   And I might feel in the warm air
> My cheek grow cold and hear the sea
> Breathe o'er my dying brain its last monotony.

"Steal" in the first line rhymes with "feel" in the second, even though these don't come at the end, and meanwhile the end words rhyme, just as there is an echo of the long *e* vowel in all these lines, including some of the end rhymes, an effect designed to suggest the sea's "monotony." Another striking example of interlinear rhyme is MacNeice's "The Sunlight on the Garden":

> Our freedom as free lances
> Advances towards its end;
> The earth compels, upon it
> Sonnets and birds descend;
> And soon, my friend,
> We shall have no time for dances.

Here the rhyming word at end position in some of the lines is directly followed by a rhyming word at the beginning of the next line. Given that rhyming at the ends of lines helps stabilize our sense of line division in a text, by the same token, interlinear internal rhyme to some degree *de*stabilizes that regular division into audibly uniform groups; and the author should have reasons for doing so—otherwise such rhyming will seem gratuitous.

A fairly common departure from the norm is the use of *light rhyme,* where a stressed syllable duplicates rhyme conditions with an *un*stressed syllable, for example:

> The shepherds' swains shall dance and sing
> For thy delight each May morning.
>
>   MARLOWE, "The Passionate Shepherd to His Love"

Light rhyme has enjoyed special favor in the twentieth century, used by the modernists in particular because it is less insistent than normative rhyme. It has a glancing quality, a leaner sound than full rhyme and satisfying for that reason to a sparer aesthetic.

Assonance is the rhyming of vowels alone, a common practice in folk poems and blues lyrics. We see its use in Dickinson's poem (1551) in lines 1–2 and 4–5:

> Those-dying then,
> Knew where they went–
> They went to God's Right Hand–
> That Hand is amputated now
> And God cannot be found–

The incomplete, assonantal rhymes might be read as reinforcing the sense of a mismatch, of separation from divine assurances; even without a signifying role, the assonantal rhymes appeal to the ear as part of the poem's dissonant texture. I'll mention, in passing, a special (and rarer) case of assonance known as *back rhyme*, where the consonant sounds *preceding* the rhyming vowel are the same, but the consonant sounds following it differ, as in "sack" and "sash," or "release" and "leaf."

Consonantal rhyme, or *consonance*, is the duplication of consonant sounds only, as in lines 3 and 5 in Dickinson's poem above, where "Hand" makes a consonantal rhyme with "found." A special form of consonance is *two-consonant rhyme*, the duplication of consonants preceding *and* following the unrhyming vowel sound, as with "dill" and "dull," or "elated" and "delighted." Wilfred Owen became something of a specialist in two-consonant rhymes as in his "Strange Meeting":

> For of my glee might many men have laughed,
> And of my weeping something had been left,
> Which must die now. I mean the truth untold,
> The pity of war, the pity war distilled.

Identical rhyme is the rhyming of a word with itself, as in Dickinson's poem "Because I could not stop for Death":

> We paused before a House that seemed
> A Swelling of the Ground—
> The Roof was scarcely visible—
> The Cornice—in the Ground—

Identical rhyme leaves the reader faintly dissatisfied or disappointed, or even bored with a repetition. Similar to it is *homophonic rhyme,* where rhyming words have identical sounds but different meanings or spellings, as "rough" with "ruff," or "distinguished" (verb) and "distinguished" (adjective). In French poetry this kind of rhyme is so common as not to count as a variant, and is known as *rime équivoque,* "equivocal rhyme," a form of rhyme that Mallarmé particularly favored.

We should note in passing that assonantal double rhymes are at least theoretically possible, as in "only" and "rosy" or even "quonset" and "hogshead." Consonantal double rhymes could also be made—for example, "thermal" and "formal," or even "dreadlock" and "toadlike"—or two-consonant double rhymes like "cowbell" and "cobble."

One fairly rare rhyme variant is what has been called, somewhat imprecisely, *apocopaic rhyme* (a term more often used as a synonym for "light rhyme"). Perhaps a better term for it would be *half-double rhyme.* This kind of rhyme is the matching of duplicate vowel and consonant sounds in a stressed syllable that rhymes, followed, in one of the rhyming words, by a weakly stressed *unrhyming* syllable. "Pure" and "during" or "restrain" and "zany" are half-double rhymes. They are used to good effect in Auden's "The Duet" and in James Merrill's "Mirror," which, for example, rhymes "gilded" with "will" and "arrangement" with "change."

An interesting variant of assonance involves rhyming consonants as well, but in reverse order. This kind of rhyming has been called *amphisbaenic,* and examples could include rhyming "late" with "tale," or "chic" with "quiche," or "zone" with "nose."

Another form of rhyme is *elided rhyme,* based on the elision of a vowel in a word with falling accent to produce a single syllable rhyming with that word—for example, rhyming "cresset" with "nest," or "fervid" with "curved." William Carlos Williams gets a nice effect using elided rhyme in "The Dance," with the difference that he changes the vowel sound as well, making what might be called a *consonantal elided rhyme:*

> When the snow falls the flakes
> spin upon the long axis

By now we are in the territory of approximate rhyme, where a number of terms are used, such as *off rhyme, near rhyme, slant rhyme,* etc. In this latitudinarian zone, similarities of sound produce rhyming pairs such as "dark/card," "drama/armor," "aspirin/inspiring," "locate/collate," and what have you. This kind of rhyme has been particularly in favor during the recent revival of interest in metered and rhymed poetry.

Rhyme helps to locate the end of a line for the ear and thus is a valuable reinforcement of meter. Its regular recurrence reaffirms expectations raised by the return of a set number of feet per line. Meter is always felt less strongly in unrhymed lines than in rhymed; for that reason, poets seeking a less artificial, more speechly medium have chosen blank verse—and have had to exercise even greater care in firmly establishing the meter so that the audience won't fail to follow it.

Rhyme also serves a function in establishing the nature of the poetic stanza; in fact, the several types of stanzas are determined by the joint interaction of the governing meter and the periodic recurrences of rhyme. In order to establish the nature of a stanza, prosody describes the sequence of rhymes using what is called a *rhyme scheme.* Each rhyme is assigned a letter of the alphabet that is repeated every time the same rhyming sounds recur. Thus, the well-known child's prayer "Now I lay me down to sleep" has a rhyme scheme of *aabb,* corresponding to the two rhyming couplets in the prayer. Or in Shakespeare's lyric from *Love's Labour's Lost,*

> When daises pied and violets blue
>   And ladysmocks all silver-white,
> And cuckoobuds of yellow hue
>   Do paint the meadows with delight,

we have a rhyme scheme of *abab.* In longer stanzas with other rhymes, the sequence continues with a new letter for each new rhyme, as many as are needed, though stanzas seldom are long enough to need rhymes that would have to be labeled beyond letter *g.*

A later chapter will take up the various poetic stanzas, but we will pause here to look at a special case that is more than usually determined by rhyme. This is the quatrain (four-line stanza) written with *analyzed rhyme,* where there are four rhyming end words, each word rhyming assonantally with one of the other words and consonantally with another. A possible sequence of analyzed rhymes would be:

> ...home
> ...tone
> ...rhyme
> ...mine

The rhyme scheme could be written either as *aabb* or *abab*, depending on whether assonance or consonance were considered the more important rhyme. Or, using numbers to stand for consonants and letters for vowels, the rhyme scheme could be notated this way and cover both aspects of the rhyme: $a(1)\ a(2)\ b(1)\ b(2)$. Analyzed rhyme may also use two-consonant rhymes, in which case sequences like the following will appear: *Rome/lone, rhyme/line.* A possible notation for the rhymes would be: $(1)a(2)\ (3)a(4)$ $(1)b(2)\ (3)b(4)$. Luckily most rhyme schemes are less complicated to notate, since they involve normative rhyming only. A potential danger of adopting formal schemes like analyzed rhyme with two-consonant rhymes is their tendency to devolve into bald displays of technical ingenuity—but then it's also possible that a sufficiently impassioned practitioner of poetic art could achieve something out of the ordinary with them.

So far we have looked at rhyme from a purely phonic standpoint. Apart from constructive euphony, rhyme has, in fact, an important semantic function in the development of a poem. The coincidence of sound in a pair of rhymes is a recommendation to the reader to consider the rhyming words in tandem, to see what meaning emerges from their juxtaposition. The meaning will emerge as one of *affinity* or of *opposition*. "Sharing" and "caring" are popular rhymes based on affinity of intention. "Breath" and "death" are timeworn rhymes of opposition. The tendency of certain key rhymes with semantic affinity to reappear in poems over and over again presents a challenge to the new poet who rhymes. Worn-out tandems like "see" and "tree," "blue" and "true," or "old" and "gold" can be used only at the risk of triteness. On the other hand, the search for fresh rhymes can lead the poet to the discovery of unexamined connections between disparate phenomena, as when Browning found this rhyme (in "Love Among the Ruins"):

> All the mountains topped with temples, all the glades'
>   Colonnades,

Generally we think of colonnades as an urban architectural feature, but here the connection between temple columns and natural tree trunks is brought to consciousness by a rhyme.

Without ever codifying them, poetic practice has established a series of guidelines as to what makes a fresh and instructive rhyme. Overfamiliar rhymes are disliked, along with rhymes where no semantic connection can be made between the two rhyming words. Just as *life/wife* is, at the semantic level, too familiar, *rhyme/lime* is meaningless (that is, until proven otherwise). Rhymes involving different parts of speech are generally prized over rhymes with the same part of speech: thus, *song/long* or *mean/green* is a more interesting rhyme than *take/shake*. Since monosyllabic rhyming quickly becomes monotonous, the competent poet will try to bring in a healthy number of rhyming words having more than one syllable. Rhymes that link words having differing numbers of syllables are considered more interesting than those that rhyme words with the *same* number of syllables. Thus, *sound/abound* has more rhythmic appeal that *gore/fore* or *penniless/wretchedness*.

Connected to the concern for varying the number of syllables in rhyme-words is the value placed on rhyming strongly stressed syllables with syllables having weaker stress—that is, at stress level 2. For example, rhyming "press" with "happiness" pairs the syllable "press" (at level 3) with "-ness" at level 2, which engages the ear. On the other hand, rhyming syllables where *both* have stress at level 2, as with *quality/embassy,* is much less satisfying than rhyming, say, "quality" with "free."

Finally, since most poems are read nowadays rather than heard, a concern for spelling differences has shaped rhyming at its most refined. It is considered more interesting to rhyme syllables that are spelled differently than those with the same spelling. Thus, *fee/agree* is slightly less interesting than *bright/neophyte.* English abounds in multiple spellings for the same sound, a fact that puts this visual refinement in rhyme within the compass of most skillful poets. On the other hand, if every rhyme is complex and unprecedented, the poem may give the impression of cleverness and artificiality.

As an instance of expert rhyming, consider the conclusion to Hardy's "The Darkling Thrush":

> So little cause for carolings
>   Of such ecstatic sound
> Was written on terrestrial things
>   Afar or nigh around,
> That I could think there trembled through
>   His happy good-night air
> Some blessed Hope, whereof he knew
>   And I was unaware.

Notice that we find only one monosyllabic pair of rhymes; otherwise all rhymes pair words of differing numbers of syllables. And rhymes are also different parts of speech, often with differently spelled rhyming syllables. Those who have the leisure should see the whole poem and then return to these concluding lines in order to speculate about semantic connections between rhyming words.

In these several distinctions, phonic or semantic, we see at work the essential principle behind rhyme: the linking of things that are at once similar and different. Where there is no similarity, there is no rhyme. Where the similarity is too great, boredom sets in. Skillful rhyming involves finding a balance between identity and difference.

5. Stanza

Just as prose writers divide their texts into paragraphs, poets in most instances divide poems of any length into separate blocks usually called *stanzas*. Stanzaic divisions of a poem normally contain the same number of lines. When they do not, some poets prefer to call the divisions *verse paragraphs*, even though such paragraphs are not usually indented: separation provided by blank space serves as sufficient marker of the division.

Another term for nonuniform divisions is *strophe*, which is derived from technical descriptions of the classical ode. In Greek and Latin poetry, an ode had no specified length, but it was always divided into three parts: strophe, antistrophe, and epode. There was no prescribed form for the strophe, but whatever disposition of lines and meters the author developed for it, the second part (the antistrophe) followed exactly. Finally, the epode (the third section) brought in another meter altogether. Because of the loosely regulated character of ode structure, some metrists have used the term "strophe" for verse paragraphs of differing lengths in a poem. It is more often used, though, to describe verses in poems set to music, hence the term "strophic song." The application in music is doubtful, given that few musical settings involve classical odes. Most often the "strophes" of a song are written with identical meter and rhyme scheme throughout (this is the case with nearly all hymns, for example), and usually there are more than two strophes in any poem set to music—still without anything resembling an epode after the two opening sections. In this book, to avoid confusion, I will restrict the technical term *strophe* to the classical ode only. Otherwise, divisions of a poem will be called *stanzas* or *verse paragraphs*.

Stanzas that do have the same number of lines, the same meter, and the same rhyme scheme, are said to be *in responsion*. Responsion is useful in determining the meter of a poem, because a single stanza may be metrically ambiguous. By consulting several stanzas in responsion, the reader can discern what prosodic directives have gone into the construction of the poem.

In Italian the word *stanza* means "room." Some poets find the metaphor of the poem as a house divided into several rooms helpful in thinking about poems. The first stanza is an entry. Then come one or more rooms for public reception. Rooms of a private character take more time and distance (or flights of stairs) to penetrate. On the other hand, we can also use "stanza" nonmetaphorically, simply as a designation for the uniform divisions of a poem. Yet it's important to ask why a poem should be divided into stanzas at all. At the simplest level, stanza divisions are like paragraphs in prose: a given subject is sectioned off into smaller, more manageable units. Each part is organized around one or two central ideas or images. When the author has said what needs to be said about that part of the argument, a new topic appears. When a poem has several stanzas, however, it's not uncommon for a sentence to begin in one stanza and continue on to the next. Just as lines can be enjambed, so can stanzas. The resistance we have to enjambment between lines is a bit stronger between stanzas. The reader should be able to find reasons why two stanzas are, in effect, being joined into a unit, why the regular division into separate compartments is being set aside. Reasons will of course have to do with what's being said in the two linked stanzas; but it's safe to say that enjambment between stanzas is less common than enjambment between lines.

Not all poems, even long ones, have stanzaic divisions. *Blank verse* (unrhymed iambic pentameter), for example, is usually presented as an unbroken column of text. It is sometimes divided into verse paragraphs of differing length, but rarely does it take the form of stanzas in responsion—though Wallace Stevens's poems are notable exceptions, including, to name one example, *Notes Toward a Supreme Fiction*. Once again, this fact about blank verse follows from its character as the least artificial form of verse, the one closest to speech or prose: regular stanza divisions would seem like an artificial intrusion into the unbroken flow of speech. On the other hand, many readers find it daunting or oppressive to be faced with a long stretch of text not interrupted by empty spaces dividing it into manageable sections. Stanzaic divisions are usually welcoming to the eye, less intimidating than the solid columns of verse that make up, say, *Paradise Lost* or *The Prelude*. It may be that the notoriously short attention span of contemporary readers makes the writing of long poems without stanzaic divisions inadvisable. Milton and Wordsworth could count on a different kind of readership. The term for poems written without stanzaic division, incidentally, is *stichic* verse from Greek *stichos*, "line."

Stanzas are labeled by the number of lines they contain. The rarest (because shortest) stanza is the *monostich stanza*, containing one line only. Stanzas of two lines are called *distichs* or *couplets.* The three-line stanza is called a *tercet,* the four-line, *quatrain,* the five, *cinquain,* the six, *sestet,* the eight, *octave,* the ten, *dizain.* Terms for other line lengths—for example, "septet" or "nonet"—are imaginable but not in common use. Instead, we say *seven-line* or *nine-line stanza,* and let it go at that.

Apart from the number of lines in the unit, a stanza's nature is determined by the rhymes it uses. A series of distichs, or couplets, may rhyme *aa, bb, cc,* and so on, indefinitely. When rhymed distichs are cast in iambic pentameter, they are called *heroic couplets,* the pattern used for almost all serious poetry in England written between 1650 and 1780. The tight, neat heroic couplet makes for an apt counterpart to the classicizing temper of this period in English literature, and those same qualities have made heroic couplets something of a rarity in the freewheeling modern era.

Possibilities begin to expand with the tercet, which may rhyme *aaa, axa, aax,* or *xaa* (where *x* stands for nonrhyming sounds). Poets have said that the tercet is an "unstable" unit, lacking the evenly balanced support felt to be present in either the couplet or the quatrain. Having only three lines to rest on makes the tercet roll forward into the next stanza and the next, rather like the continuous belted traction of a tank or earth-mover. Movement may be slow or headlong, but it is always forward, and thus tercets help draw the reader through long poems. They are, moreover, sometimes linked by rhyme in what is called *concatenation,* which produces a series as follows: *aba bcb cdc,* and so on, the series coming to a close by a sequence of rhymes as follows: *xyz yzyz.* This collaboration of tercet stanza with interlocking rhyme is called *terza rima* ("third rhyme"). Dante, the great fourteenth-century Italian poet, invented it and used it in his *Divine Comedy*. Terza rima hasn't very often been adopted in English because of the difficulty of finding, over and over again in a long sequence, three unforced rhyming words. Shelley's "Ode to the West Wind" is perhaps the most famous English poem in terza rima, but his *The Triumph of Life* also uses it effectively. The concatenated rhymes add to the strong forward impetus of tercets in general, an effect which, again, makes terza rima useful in narrative poems. It also seems to encourage the construction of long sentences with elaborate syntax, arranged in arresting ways across the lines. No one with only moderate technical skill should attempt it.

Lyrics in English are most often written in quatrains. Rhyming may run *abab*, forming what is called the *Sicilian quatrain* (because it is said to have been invented in Sicily), or *abba*, which forms the *Tuscan* or *Italian quatrain*, named, again, because of its presumed origin. The Italian quatrain is also often called the *envelope stanza* because two external rhymes "envelop" the internal couplet. Another possibility in quatrains is the two-couplet scheme *aabb*, though of course this is less cohesive than the other arrangements: couplet quatrains tend to break in half, registering more strongly as couplets than as quatrains. In general, quatrains adapt well to the lyric and are frequently set to music. Each unit exhibits a foursquare completeness that in itself adds to an overall sense of security or stability.

Very sensitive poets will use the given rhyme scheme of the quatrain as a constitutive element in the meaning of the poem. The Sicilian quatrain holds the suggestion of making a move or taking a step, *a* to *b,* repeating the process for the last two lines of the quatrain, and so with each quatrain in the poem, over and over again, concluding with a final transfer from *y* to *z.* The implication is one of definite change or progress, reiterated many times. Meanwhile the envelope stanza suggests moving from one vantage point, *a,* to another, *b,* staying there temporarily, and then returning to the point of departure *a.* In this scheme, the internal couplet is sometimes felt as, so to speak, the message in the bottle, a self-contained unit held in the protective or oppressive embrace of the external rhymes. Suppose we look at specific examples with these categories in mind.

First, a Sicilian quatrain:

> There is not room for Death,
> Nor atom that his might could render void
> Since thou art Being and Breath,
> And what thou art may never be destroyed.
>
> EMILY BRONTË, "No Coward Soul Is Mine"

Here the threat to eternal life is raised in line one only to be immediately dismissed; in line two, Death's ineffectual power finds a concrete illustration: it cannot annihilate so much as a single atom. A parallel pair of lines follows, presenting the same movement toward security and salvation in positive terms: God is all of life and being, and, therefore, every part of God is safe from destruction.

Here is an Italian quatrain:

> Meanwhile, the men, with vestiges of pomp,
> Race memories of king and caravan,
> High-priests, an ostrich, and a juju-man,

Go singing through the footpaths of the swamp.

JEAN TOOMER, "Georgia Dusk"

The quatrain begins by representing African-American workmen in the present, in touch with only part of their lost heritage. Line two brings in the memories of the African past, which line three dwells on momentarily. In the last line we are brought back to the present, an unidealized Southern American landscape. "Pomp" has been replaced by the swamp, with only a few vestiges of the regal past remaining.

The cinquain is not very common in our poetry because it is less stable than the quatrain or sestet and doesn't fall into rhyme schemes that seem inevitable. Schemes like *ababa* or *abbab* strike us as quatrains with an extra, confusing limb; they also add the difficulty of finding three functional rhyme words. If a *c* rhyme is introduced, one of the lines will necessarily remain unrhymed. For these reasons, the cinquain is best reserved for poems with subjects that are in some sense skewed or hindered.

Meanwhile, the sestet may be thought of as an intermediate stanza, longer than the quatrain without having the full solidity of the octave. A common rhyme scheme for the sestet is *ababcc,* three pairs of rhymes arranged as a Sicilian quatrain followed by a couplet, which gives a feeling of closure at the stanza's end. Other schemes are possible as well — for example, *abbacc,* an Italian quatrain followed by a couplet. In this case couplet closure registers less strongly because there are *two* couplets, one coming before the stanza's conclusion.

The sestet is sometimes rhymed *abccba,* which (even more than the Italian quatrain) gives an impression of steps taken in one direction and then retraced to a point of origin. The opposite sense can be given by using rhymes in the series *abcabc,* a reiterative pattern always forward in motion but with a faint sense of rote activity—like learning the abc's. A slight modification produces the rhyme scheme *abcbac,* an order that gives the sense of reaching a certain point, backtracking a bit, and then returning to the extreme forward point again. It would fit well with narratives or "arguments" that recount a departure from home base, followed by second thoughts or retreat, followed by firmed-up resolve to push on.

A well-known stanza form for the seven-line stanza is *rhyme royal,* which has the scheme *ababbcc.* It has only one set of three rhymes, which is a challenge but not an invincible one. Chaucer wrote several poems in rhyme royal, including the long narrative *Troylus and Criseyde* and shorter lyrics like "Trouthe." The effect of rhyme royal is to move from looseness and complexity toward strictness and clarity, concluding as it does with two sets of rhyming couplets, the opening rhyme of the first couplet also serving as the concluding rhyme of an initial Sicilian quatrain. Auden used this stanza for his long poem "A Letter to Lord Byron," which bears a resemblance to Byron's own *Don Juan.* That poem, though, was written in a slightly more difficult stanza that we are about to look at.

Octaves are often composed of two joined quatrains, either Italian or Sicilian, or one of each. But the most renowned octave stanza is *ottava rima* ("eighth rhyme"), which was used for several epic poems beginning with Ariosto's *Orlando Furioso,* and then Tasso's *Gerusalemme liberata,* then Camões's *Os Lusiadas,* and, in the

Romantic period, Byron's *Don Juan.* Ottava rima requires two sets of three rhymes in alternating sequence followed by a couplet, as follows: *ababababcc.* Our language's rhyming resources are strained by the stanza, and one of the reasons that Byron managed it successfully is that *Don Juan* is a comic poem and many of the rhymes are of the "mosaic" sort discussed in the previous chapter, rhymes that almost always make us laugh. Ottava rima is often associated with cerebral or witty writing—stylish, amusing, polished. Few poets writing in English have had the technical ingenuity required to make it work, Byron being the great exception.

The dizain can be constructed by welding several other stanzas together in one unit of ten lines, but its best-known form is the one used by several sixteenth-century French poets, in particular by poet Maurice Scève in his long poem *Délie.* Scève's dizain had the rhyme scheme *ababbccdcd.* Here again, two sets of three rhymes are needed to complete the stanza, and for that reason it has seldom been used in English, even though the disposition of the rhymes—which come in a kind of mirrored order—makes for a serenely balanced effect.

Most stanzas are *isometric,* meaning that their lines all have the same number of metrical feet. Some stanzas are *heterometric,* having lines with varying numbers of feet. If we glance back to the quatrain of Emily Brontë quoted earlier, we see that it is heterometric; the first and third lines are trimeter, the second and fourth, pentameter. The reader senses this difference even before stopping to count feet in each line. After hearing a few stanzas, the alternation of short and long lines becomes part of reader expectations, a metrical tension that gives a certain urgency to the poem.

The best-known heterometric stanza is the *ballad*, which has the rhyme scheme *abcb*, with lines one and three written in tetrameter, and lines two and four in trimeter. Lines two and four rhyme, but not lines one and three. Numberless folk songs have been written in this stanza, but it is also the stanza of Coleridge's *The Rime of the Ancient Mariner*, and Dickinson used it in hundreds of her poems as well. Two interesting modern instances of the ballad stanza are Elizabeth Bishop's "The Burglar of Babylon" and James Merrill's "The Summer People." For modern ears it has a faintly comic or quaint sound, based on its insistent meter and its association with folk poems.

Another heterometric stanza, quite the opposite in its connotations, is the *Spenserian stanza*, devised by Edmund Spenser for *The Faerie Queene*. It is a nine-line stanza rhyming *ababbcbcc*, the first eight lines in iambic pentameter, the last an alexandrine (i.e., a hexameter). It was used by the Romantic poets as well—by Byron in *Childe Harold's Pilgrimage* and Keats in *The Eve of St. Agnes*. Note that it contains two couplets, one internal and the other, closural; but even more striking is the concluding hexameter, which adds weight (and metrical surprise) to the stanza's conclusion.

Heterometric stanzas are sometimes invented by a poet in what are called *nonce forms*, stanzas made up for one poem only, without following any preset models such as Sicilian quatrain or ottava rima. George Herbert composed an abundance of such heterometric poems—for example, his "Praise (3)":

Lord, I will mean and speak thy praise,
Thy praise alone.
My busy heart shall spin it all my days:
And when it stops for want of store,
Then will I wring it with a sigh or groan,
That thou mayst yet have more.

The poem continues with six further stanzas, all in responsion to this one. Their rhyme scheme is *abacbc,* but, in addition, line one is written in tetrameter, line two in dimeter, line three in pentameter, line four in tetrameter, line five in pentameter, and line six in trimeter. Note as well that Herbert makes his indentations of the lines correspond to the meter: the pentameter lines are flush left, and the single dimeter line is indented the farthest right. The two tetrameter lines are indented the same distance from the left margin in order to correspond spatially; and the final trimeter stands a bit farther to the right than they. Plotting indentation on the page helps establish congruence of meter so that we can comprehend the stanza's structure, with this same pattern reproduced throughout the poem. As far as I know this stanza is truly a "nonce form," never used again by Herbert nor any later poet, though it is always possible someone may adapt it for new purposes. All stanzas must originally have been "nonce forms," but some of them came into general use because of the expressive opportunities and felicities they offered.

6. Verseforms

Some poems follow a fixed format that coordinates more than one of the following features: the meter, the number of lines, stanzaic division, and rhyme scheme. These formats are called *verseforms*. Some stanzas are written according to a prescribed format, too, as we saw in the last chapter. For example, the Sicilian quatrain contains four lines (in whatever meter) rhymed *abab*. But the number of lines for a poem composed with this kind of quatrain is *not* prescribed: the poem may contain any number of such quatrains. By contrast, a verseform has a fixed number of lines, as well as a fixed rhyme scheme. (Verseforms, almost universally, involve rhyming.) The limerick, for example, is a five-line verseform, and the line requirement never changes; if the number of lines were changed, you would have a different animal. (The one exception to this rule seems to be the sonnet. In strict terms, the sonnet must have fourteen lines; but tradition includes a few variants on the form written with more than fourteen lines, or fewer. The sonnet also includes rhymes according to one classic pattern, but variations on that pattern have also been developed over the centuries, as will be outlined a few paragraphs ahead.)

We might pause a moment to reflect on the purpose and scope of verseforms. A poem in a verseform is almost invariably less than two pages long, and, more often, less than a page long. The sestina, for example, comprises thirty-nine lines, and the ballade (as distinct from the ballad), twenty-eight. These are among the longest verseforms. The inference to draw is that verseforms have a narrower scope than the open-ended poem in blank verse (or in tercets or quatrains), which can reach epic length. Verseforms are associated with the lyric, the satire, the fable, the meditative poem—and only occasionally with narrative.

The decision to write a poem according to a prescribed pattern is based on the assumption that the subject allows for a high level of control. The author doesn't decide how long to make the poem: the verseform decides. For example, if the author can't say all there is to say in fourteen lines about the subject, then the poem can't be written as a sonnet. To choose a verseform for a poem suggests that the poet is willing to accept the impersonal assistance (and regulation) of a fixed formal structure. This structure rules out a spontaneous, improvisational approach, and that is its drawback. On the other hand, the verseform stands as an emblem of abstract order, with the implication that the shapeless flux of experience has the potential of being contained in preexistent formal patterns. Many readers find these patterns beautiful in themselves—as the hexagonal form of a snowflake or the design of a catenary suspension bridge is beautiful. There is no mistaking the pleasure arising from the discovery of a form capable of coinciding with experience that would otherwise have no special shape. This pleasure is part of the "magic" aspect of poetry; the surprising arrangements achieved in verseform make us regard the poet able to make them as possessed of special powers unavailable to most people. Even if no special magic or occult powers are actually involved, then at least virtuosity is. I think most people would acknowledge that virtuosity, though far from being the greatest value in art, is nevertheless a real value. If we dislike the connotations of the word, then we can substitute for it "skill," "craft," or "mastery." Wordsworth says that successfully managed poetic form appeals to us with "the sense of difficulty overcome," a sense that is both reassuring and pleasurable. The admiration an audience feels for an effectively written ballade, say, is comparable to the admiration stirred by a dancer performing a solo that required years of training to achieve; or by an aria only someone with superior vocal talent and training could begin to sing; or by an Olympic skier who successfully completes a complicated, zigzag course down the slopes. Achievements like these demonstrate to us that human effort can sometimes raise ordinary abilities to a new level of competence and brilliance and so serve as models for succeeding at other challenges beyond routine competence.

The first task facing the poet who wishes to write in a verseform is to study the best poems that have used it; the tension between being *like* earlier examples of the form and *unlike* them is an important aspect of the compositional process. When Romantic individualists object to verseforms on the grounds that using a structure devised by another artist is an unacceptable encroachment on originality and the free play of the imagination, the best rebuttal is simply to point to the tradition in all its contrasting variety. When we examine all the approaches poets have taken to any given prosodic structure, we can't fail to see that it highlights (instead of suppressing) individual differences between poets.

To grasp the scope and potential of verseforms, suppose we look at the sonnet, in the English language the best known verseform of all. Historians speculate that it began sometime in the thirteenth century, when early experimenters joined two Sicilian quatrains with two tercets to compose a fourteen-line form with a strongly marked division between the first eight lines (known as the *octave*) and the concluding six (known as the *sestet*). Giacomo da Lentini is credited with producing this early form of the sonnet, whose meter was hendecasyllabic (having eleven syllables) and whose rhyme scheme was *abababab cdecde*. Later in the thirteenth century Guittone d'Arezzo substituted Italian quatrains for the octave, giving it the rhyme scheme *abbaabba*, which became standard for Italian poetry, after Dante and Petrarch had both used it. Other Romance languages followed the Italian lead, and so, eventually, did English poetry.

Notice that the octave of the Italian sonnet contains two envelope stanzas in succession and that it also contains another envelope quatrain right at the center, the one discernible by the rhymes *baab*. These interlocking quatrains make for a high degree of sonic cohesiveness in the octave. The sestet, however, is less cohesive, nor does it always follow the format *cdecde*. Other possibilities in common use include *cdcdcd, cddccd, cdeedc, cdedec* — some of these encompassing rhymes that could be seen as making up an envelope quatrain. The best sonneteers in the tradition have been conscious of the implications of variant schemes in the sestet and used them expressively.

Whatever the rhyme scheme of the sestet, the Italian sonnet is at least always based on the marked division between the two parts of the verseform, which was meant to coincide with a division in the "argument" of the poem. The octave states and develops a thesis; the sestet reverses or modifies that thesis, and it does so more quickly than the octave since it has less room in which to make its counterstatement. The point in the sonnet where argument shifts was known as the *volta* ("turn"), with the sestet of course bringing in new emotions and new rhyming words, according to a different pattern. Typically the sestet is livelier, more urgent than the reflective octave; and it has the burden of concluding the poem in a way that somehow takes the octave into account without duplicating its content. Just to get an idea of the principles involved, let's look at Milton's Italian sonnet "How Soon Hath Time":

> How soon hath Time, the subtle thief of youth,
>> Stoln on his wing my three and twentieth year!
>> My hasting days fly on with full career,
>> But my late spring no bud or blossom shew'th.
> Perhaps my semblance might deceive the truth,
>> That I to manhood am arrived so near,
>> An inward ripeness doth much less appear,
>> That some more timely-happy spirits endu'th.
> Yet be it less or more, or soon or slow,
>> It shall be still in strictest measure even
>> To that same lot, however mean or high,
> Toward which Time leads me, and the will of Heaven;
>> All is, if I have grace to use it so,
>> As ever in my great Taskmaster's eye.

Milton uses two Italian quatrains for the octave and a sestet with the rhyme scheme *cdedce*. To make the formal divisions of the sonnet more apparent, he indents lines following those divisions; yet all lines are written in iambic pentameter. The octave states the poem's central concern, which is really a lament: Milton has arrived at his twenty-third year and has produced no "bud or blossom" of achievement. The idea of having lost one's youth at the age of twenty-three was less startling in the seventeenth century, when few people lived past forty and many died before age thirty. The "volta" or "turn" is announced by "Yet" in line nine, introducing a sestet that tries to find alleviating arguments for the poet's distress. Even if the speaker has no external proof of "inward ripeness," he will nevertheless submit to the decrees of Heaven; he promises to make his maturity match the level of his circumstances, whether high or low. ("Even" in this context means "equal to," "on a par with.") The poet's resolve to be adequate to his place in the course of life, and his awareness of divine grace, allow him to accept his condition as it is at this moment. God the Taskmaster nevertheless forgives apprentices who have as yet little to show.

Italian sonnets do not conclude with a rhyming couplet, but when Thomas Wyatt brought the form over into English in the sixteenth century, he often composed sestets with the rhyme scheme *cddcee*. The prominent rhymes of the final couplet served to underline closure in the poem, tying it up, so to speak, in a neat bow. Later English Renaissance poets developed two other variants of sonnet form, both of these also concluding in a couplet. First, there was Spenser's, which has the rhyme scheme *ababbcbccdcdee*. In the Spenserian sonnet, the sharp distinction between the octave and sestet is blurred because the *c* rhyme opening the sestet has already appeared in the octave; moreover, the *babbcb* sequence established in the octave occurs—with new rhymes—again (as *cbccdc*), beginning in the octave and concluding in the sestet; it does not immediately yield to a new pattern and new rhymes peculiar to the second part of the poem. The reader may also feel that the concluding couplet has a less strong closural effect, considering that two couplets have already appeared in the poem, one in the octave and one in the sestet. On the other hand, the pattern makes us expect the *d* rhyme to follow in the same sequence established for the rhymes involving *b* and *c*; but instead the *ee* couplet disrupts the sequence, with undeniable closural force. What is, in fact, distinctive about the Spenserian sonnet is its interlocking *b* and *c* rhymes, which, by rising to a virtuosic total of four and extending across six lines, hold the entire form tightly together in a cohesive stream of argument. To see Spenser's form in action look at his Sonnet 70:

> Fresh spring the herald of love's mighty king,
> In whose coat armour richly are displayed
> All sorts of flowers the which on earth do spring
> In goodly colours gloriously arrayed.
> Go to my love, where she is careless laid,
> Yet in her winter's bower not well awake:
> Tell her the joyous time will not be stayed
> Unless she do him by the forelock take.
> Bid her therefore herself soon ready make,
> To wait on love amongst his lovely crew:
> Where every one that misseth then her make,

Shall be by him amearst with penance due.
Make haste therefore, sweet love, whilst it is prime,
For none can call again the passèd time.

(Note that in Spenser's diction, "coat armour" means "coat of arms," "misseth" means "fails to join," "make" in line eleven means "mate," "amearst" means "punished," and "prime" means "spring.")

Better known than Spenser's sonnet is the *Elizabethan sonnet*, also termed the *Shakespearian sonnet*, after its most famous practitioner. The Elizabethan sonnet has the rhyme scheme *ababcdcdefefgg*. It solves the practical problem of overstrained rhyming resources, a serious problem in English as compared to the Romance languages. On the other hand, this variant destroys the octave/sestet division—though perhaps we should say it offers no formal *support* for that division, even though many Elizabethan sonnets include a "turn" in the argument at line nine. More appropriate *formally* for the Elizabethan sonnet is an argument that the poet wants to make three times in succession (in each of the Sicilian quatrains), and then top off with a two-line conclusion affirming or summing up the overall argument. (Yet the poet will also, occasionally, make a sudden contrary assertion to what has been said in the first twelve lines, a reversal that results in a more startling conclusion.) For an example of the three-phased argument in quatrains, plus couplet conclusion, look at Shakespeare's "That Time of Year Thou Mayst in Me Behold" (Sonnet 73). In this sonnet, Shakespeare describes three separate instances of expiration or dissolution in nature—the winter season, the sunset hour, and the

dying down of a fire. After these repetitions have firmly estab-
lished the theme of mortality, a final couplet addresses the poet's
beloved with this conclusion: "This thou perceiv'st, which makes
thy love more strong, / To love that well which thou must leave ere
long." Many critics have found the sonically insistent couplet
annoying, particularly when it coincides with an abstract, moral-
izing conclusion. Yet the example of Shakespeare's sonnets has
been so powerful that roughly half of all sonnets in English are
cast in this variant form.

Actually, we have many other sonnet variants in English. There
is, for example, Shelley's "Ozymandias," written with the rhyme
scheme *ababacdcedefef,* which keeps some of the formal reinforce-
ment of the octave/sestet distinction as well as avoiding the con-
cluding couplet. We might also look at Keats's "On the Sonnet,"
which rhymes *abcabdcabcdede.* It has the cohesiveness of the Spen-
serian sonnet while making fewer demands on rhyming resources;
and it, too, avoids the insistent final couplet rhymes. Dante Gabriel
Rossetti, while writing Italian sonnets in English, nevertheless
retained the Elizabethan final couplet by writing sestets with the
rhyme scheme *cdcdee.* His concluding couplets are less moralizing
than most of Shakespeare's, though, and generally well integrated
into the main argument of the poem, and so the couplet stands
out less glaringly.

Occasionally poets have reversed the order of the sonnet,
beginning with the sestet and concluding with the octave, but this
form will seem appropriate only to a subject that begins with a
greater concentration and then relaxes into expanded discursive-
ness just before the halfway point. Now and then poets have put

the two tercets in the middle of the form, so that we have quatrain, tercet, tercet, quatrain; and, even more rarely, tercet, quatrain, quatrain, tercet. These forms divide the sonnet exactly in half and so require a subject that divides just as evenly.

There are a few examples, too, of what is called a *double sonnet*, with sixteen line in the first section and twelve in the second. The double sonnet is reserved for those subjects that need more room for the development of an argument and counterargument than is provided for in the standard fourteen lines. The main difficulty with the double sonnet is avoiding an impression of undue length, an argument elaborated in too great detail.

Since we are now discussing variants at a considerable remove from the standard sonnet, note that some critics regard the sixteen-line stanza that George Meredith used in his long narrative *Modern Love* a sonnet variant. Each section of the poem consists of four Italian quatrains joined together as a single stanza, this slightly expanded format allowing for the convenient deployment of verse narrative. Meredith's subject is love, the hallowed theme of the sonnet sequence, which in general records the narrative of at least the poet's feelings, however scant its coverage of external events. Sometimes sonnet sequences are given an overall title (for example, Spenser's *Amoretti*) and sometimes not (for example, Shakespeare's sonnets). In the twentieth century, authors as disparate as Edna St. Vincent Millay and John Berryman have published sonnet sequences; and James Merrill has written several longer poems in which the sonnet serves as a kind of stanza in an extended narrative.

As a conclusion, I will mention another sonnet variant, with only eleven lines total. This is that *curtal sonnet*, devised by Gerard

Manley Hopkins. It has the rhyme scheme *abcabcdbcdc,* the first ten lines written in iambic pentameter, the last line a single spondee. Hopkins's best-known poem in the form is "Pied Beauty," and the form has had few exponents after him. We can see that it is a sonnet only "by courtesy," and perhaps the same can be said for other variants such as the *heroic sonnet,* an eighteen-line form, or the *caudated sonnet,* which has twenty lines. Interested students may look up the precise requirements for these variants in Lewis Turco's *The Book of Forms* (see Selected Bibliography), which offers an exhaustive catalogue of common and rare verseforms in several language traditions.

In all cases, sonnet variants must demonstrate that they are the best vehicle for the subject being treated; otherwise their idiosyncratic features will seem a distraction. The reader tends to dislike or read only with bemused detachment a verseform that behaves like a Rube Goldberg machine. With verseforms, as with all technical aspects in poetry writing, a fine balance must be maintained between skill and ostentatious craft. In this chapter, we've made a close examination of the sonnet, the verseform used more often than any other in English poetry. There remain a few other verseforms worth considering in detail; but, in order to understand them, we must first look at a prosodic feature known as *refrain,* which is a component in those forms.

7. Refrain

One way of looking at the difference between prose and poetry is that the latter exhibits *patterning* to a much higher degree than the former. Patterning above all makes itself felt by recurrent features of language, features that reappear at more or less exact intervals in a given text. When syllabic stresses in the opening line of a poem recur in regular alternation between weak and strong, the result registers with the listener as a significant aural pattern, which, in most poems, reappears again and again in all subsequent lines. Likewise, when certain sounds are repeated at the ends of lines through the use of rhyme, there also the recurrence is felt as a significant patterning. Finally, when a word, line, or group of lines reappears several times during the unfolding of a literary text, the audience instinctively responds to the repetition as a feature contributing to the expressive structure of the whole.

Words, lines, or stanzas repeated verbatim at regular intervals throughout a poem are called *refrains,* from Latin *refractus,* "a thing broken again," i.e., "a returning fragment." (The origin of this noun shouldn't be confused with the verb "refrain," which comes from the French *refréner,* "to restrain"; by mere linguistic accident, these two words have become homonyms in English.) Refrains are common in folk song as well as composed art songs, where they are often called the "chorus," with the implication that the audience joins the soloist for that part of the song. In liturgical chant or litanies, recurrent phrases or sentences are often arranged in this same antiphonal manner, where leader and congregation make alternate responses, sung or spoken. As such, refrains appeal to our liking for pattern as pure abstraction and for its incantatory potential as well. Refrains have an almost hypnotic quality, dragging us along with them through the power of rhythmic repetition. Nursery rhymes, fight songs, and cheerleading chants all use refrains as a structural component, and for good reason. Poets have adapted them, too, applying as much conscious art to their deployment as possible. In the most skillful applications, the meaning of the repeated word, line, or stanza gradually expands during the course of the poem. A poem achieves this effect either by making small alterations in the refrain or by placing it in several different contexts that throw light on different implications contained in it. Refrains are sometimes light and cheerful rather than profound, as with Elizabethan singing syllables like "fa-la-la-la-la" or "hey nonny nonny no," but they can be darkly ominous, a famous example being Poe's "Quoth the raven, 'Nevermore,'" in "The Raven." At the same time, because of their artificial aspect, they lend themselves to parody and are a regular feature of poems that mock the solemnity of traditional versification. One of the problems facing a poet who uses refrains in a serious context is the risk of making an unintentionally parodic impression.

Still, the refrain has important formal functions—supporting the sense of continuation and progression in a poem as we've already noted, but also helping to reinforce the effect of final closure. As long as the refrain recurs verbatim, we know that the poem is increasing its length in regular installments, and we expect more of these to appear. Therefore, when the refrain recurs with a large, unprecedented alteration in its phrasing, the change signals to us that we have come to the end of the poem. In George Herbert's "The Pearl," for example, each of the first three stanzas concludes with the phrase "Yet I love thee." At the end of the fourth and final stanza, however, the refrain is revised so that it becomes "And climb to thee"—bringing the poem to a close.

Refrains are often used in nonce forms like Herbert's poem just mentioned, Spenser's "Prothalamion," Blake's "The Lamb," Tennyson's "The Lady of Shalott," or Kipling's "Tommy"; in all these cases, refrains add a songlike and sometimes a folklike quality to the poem, moving it away from ordinary speech toward something more incantatory. It is as though the refrain contains an obsessive thought or concern, one returning over and over again to consciousness until some kind of resolution is reached and the poem ends. Here is a refrain poem by Thomas Wyatt, titled "Forget Not Yet":

> Forget not yet the tried intent
> Of such a truth as I have meant;
> My great travail so gladly spent
>   Forget not yet.
>
> Forget not yet when first began
> The weary life ye know, since when
> The suit, the service none tell can;
>   Forget not yet.
>
> Forget not yet the great assays,
> The cruel wrong, the scornful ways,

> The painful patience in denays,
>   Forget not yet.
>
> Forget not yet, forget not this,
> How long ago hath been and is
> The mind that never meant amiss;
>   Forget not yet.
>
> Forget not then thine own approved,
> That which so long hath thee so loved,
> Whose steadfast faith yet never moved;
>   Forget not this.

(In Wyatt's diction, "assays" means "trials," and "denays," "denials.") In this poem the refrain "Forget not yet" both introduces and closes each stanza, with an anxious, almost despairing entreaty, as though the speaker believed there was every chance the audience *would* forget his service and the injustice done to him. Repeating the refrain so insistently betrays the speaker's despairing mood. As with certain mental disorders, the speaker is compelled to repeat a phrase endlessly, or almost endlessly. Notice that the refrain introducing the last stanza is slightly changed, which helps us to perceive that we are coming to the end; and the final line revises the refrain to "Forget not this," as a signal that the poem (or "this") has come to an end, with a final plea to the listener to recall shared love and the record thereof in poetry.

Refrains may appear ad libitum in a poem, but they are also indispensable features of certain verseforms, in which the interval of recurrence is prescribed in advance. One of the best known of verseforms using refrain is the *villanelle,* a French form that began originally as a peasant dance and was later refined into a literary medium of considerable sophistication. The form's requirements were at first quite loosely defined, but a sixteenth-century French poet named Jean Passerat wrote a nineteen-line version that soon became the standard format followed by all practitioners. Passerat's version is based on not one but two separate rhyming refrains that recur at set intervals throughout the poem, arranged in tercets with new lines. Throughout the nineteen lines of the poem, there are only two rhyme sounds, but then of course eight of the lines are repeated refrains. The upshot is that to fulfill the form, you need, in addition to the two refrain lines in *a,* five new rhymes in *a;* and a total of six rhymes in *b.* Finding natural rhymes for the form is in itself a challenge, and English villanelles often use rhyme variants to get their full complement. A schema of the verseform is given in the stanza outlines below, with refrains represented by uppercase letter *A,* numbered 1 and 2 respectively, the lowercase letters standing for new rhymes. The verseform is made up of five tercets and a concluding quatrain in which both refrains appear consecutively, marking the close of the poem. In schematic form, with slashes marking line ends:

Stanza 1:   A1 (first refrain)| b | A2 (second refrain)
"   2:   a | b | A1
"   3:   a | b | A2
"   4:   a | b | A1
"   5:   a | b | A2
"   6:   a | b | A1 | A2.

We can flesh out this schema by citing Auden's villanelle "If I Could Tell You":

Time will say nothing but I told you so,
Time only knows the price we have to pay;
If I could tell you I would let you know.

If we should weep when clowns put on their show,
If we should stumble when musicians play,
Time will say nothing but I told you so.

There are no fortunes to be told, although,
Because I love you more than I can say,
If I could tell you I would let you know.

The winds must come from somewhere when they blow,
There must be reasons why the leaves decay;
Time will say nothing but I told you so.

Perhaps the roses really want to grow,
The vision seriously intends to stay;
If I could tell you I would let you know.

Suppose the lions all get up and go,
And all the brooks and soldiers run away;
Will Time say nothing but I told you so?
If I could tell you I would let you know.

A form incorporating refrains is a logical choice for a poem whose theme is the passage of time: the refrains' regular recurrence reminds us that a clock is ticking along as a background to whatever else may be happening. The first of the paired refrains in this poem sets up an implied dialogue between Time and human beings, and the second establishes another dialogue between two people in particular, by using the pronouns "I" and "you." Only in the third tercet is the amorous nature of the "I-you" relationship established, and the contest between Time and Love is one of poetry's oldest themes. The fifth tercet suggests that the love being treated is still in its early stages, before the persons involved know whether or not the relationship will be temporary or permanent. Actually, the concluding quatrain unmistakably raises the possibility that the relationship will end. A note of fear and exasperation is struck in the conclusion when the first refrain is revised into a question, "Will Time say nothing but I told you so?" The answer is the second refrain, which is not so much an answer as a restatement of the speaker's inability to forecast the future; but since this negation concludes the poem, the overall feeling is less than hopeful. The speaker's goodwill is darkened by the realization that Time and process erode all things, the only available human defense a stoic will to achieve some kind of wisdom that stands apart from Time's ravages.

Enacted in the concluding quatrain is an important feature of the villanelle—refrains heretofore separated by one or more lines throughout the poem at last appear consecutively. The villanelle can be thought of as the "story" that explains the final juxtaposition of the two refrains. In Auden's poem and in the best villanelles, we experience the poem as a developing or unfolding argument or plot; repetitions do not recur mechanically but in fact expand and deepen as they appear in fresh contexts. Sometimes, as in Theodore Roethke's "The Waking" or Elizabeth Bishop's

"One Art," the refrains are revised with each recurrence, making explicit the development of the poet's thought. This approach (usually termed *incremental repetition*) also has the advantage of sparing the reader the monotony of verbatim repetition and thus seeming a bit less artificial. This is a good solution so long as the revisions don't strike the reader as merely an easy way out of syntactical or prosodic tangles. With the villanelle, as with all verseforms, the illusion of ease and inevitability should be the goal.

Another form incorporating a refrain is the *ballade*, developed to a high degree of perfection by fourteenth- and fifteenth-century French poets such as Christine de Pisan, Charles d'Orléans, and François Villon. It was adapted for English poetry by Chaucer (in several variant guises), as well as by Charles d'Orléans in his English-language work, but was mostly neglected after that until the late nineteenth century, when French verseforms enjoyed a vogue among minor English poets of the day. In the twentieth century we have free adaptations of it by Ezra Pound ("Villonaud for This Yule") and recent examples by Richard Wilbur ("Ballade for the Duke of Orléans"), James Merrill ("The Help" and "Snow Jobs"), and Marilyn Hacker ("Ballad of Ladies Lost and Found," an extended variant of the form).

In French poetry the twenty-eight lines of the ballade were octosyllabic, the whole consisting of three eight-line stanzas, each with the rhyme scheme *ababbcbC*, where the uppercase *C* represents the refrain line. The form concluded with a four-line *envoi* (or *envoy*), with the rhyme scheme *bcbC*, and including a final repetition of the refrain. The special difficulty for poets writing in English is finding enough rhyming words—only three rhyme sounds for the whole poem—to complete the form without an apparent sense of strain. Most attempting it have made the shift from octosyllabics to iambic pentameter, which lightens the burden a little (though James Merrill's "Snow Jobs" is in iambic tetrameter). The ballade is never narrative; rather it sustains a meditative mode in which a given subject is turned over and regarded from several angles, with the refrain appearing four times, as though it were an inexorable decree handed down by Fate. However far the poem's reflections extend, they always return to the refrain, a fact that, along with the insistent rhyming, lends the form a feeling of stoicism in the face of iron constraint. Because of its difficulty, the ballade was often a contest piece in late medieval France, an occasion to demonstrate technical brilliance in competition with other poets. And yet in the hands of a Villon it could become a cosmic survey of the human condition in all its terror and pathos. No ballade as great as Villon's has yet been written in English, if for no other reason than the almost insuperable problem of finding a sufficient number of rhymes without seeming to strain for them.

A special case of verseform based on refrain is the *sestina*, which calls for repetition not of whole lines but of six terminal words. Arnaut Daniel, a Provençal poet of the late twelfth century, is usually credited with inventing it, but many others have excelled in the form, including Dante, Petrarch, Camões, Sir Philip Sidney, Swinburne, Pound, John Ashbery, Mona Van Duyn, and Anthony Hecht. The thirty-nine lines of the poem are constituted by six stanzas of six lines each, plus a concluding envoy (or *tornada*) of three lines. Each line ends with one of six controlling words, which recur in a fixed order as follows:

First stanza:	1 2 3 4 5 6
Second stanza:	6 1 5 2 4 3
Third stanza:	3 6 4 1 2 5
Fourth stanza:	5 3 2 6 1 4
Fifth stanza:	4 5 1 3 6 2
Sixth stanza:	2 4 6 5 3 1
Envoy:	5 3 1 or 1 3 5.

There is usually another requirement concerning the envoy: the other end words 2, 4, and 6 should appear somewhere in the three concluding lines.

Complicated? Yes, but the challenge has seemed irresistible to many poets, and some great poems have been done in this verse-form, including Dante's so-called "Stony Sestina," and Philip Sidney's *double sestina,* twice as long as the conventional one, titled "Ye Goatherd Gods." In English, we can note that the best examples of sestina use one or two refrain words that have falling rhythm, like "forests" or "valleys," which adds a little accentual variety to the poem and helps reduce the risk of monotony. Sestinas characteristically deal with obsessive or dreamlike states of mind, where key words return to be reconsidered over and over. The effect can be a bit claustrophobic, but by the same token it can also be funny, and the form can be credited with scoring a number of comic successes. Some, like Elizabeth Bishop's "Sestina" blend comic and sad components together to achieve a special tone that, deployed in this hypnotic verseform, casts a particular spell over the reader. There is something ritualistic about the sestina, reinforcing our half-conscious notion of the poet as a sort of shaman with quasi-magical powers. Possible pitfalls include those risked whenever we attempt a form as rigidly controlled as this: a sense of strain, the resort to padding, a static or monotonous overall impression. The poet seeking to avoid such pitfalls must call on the widest and deepest technical skills in order to shape a poem that seems natural and inevitable, with a strong sense of progression throughout and a strong conclusion.

8. Quantitative Verse

In chapter 1, we looked at other metrical systems and noted that Greek and Latin poetry were written in *quantitative meter,* a system using syllable length rather than stress as the metrical base. For poetry in Greek, a long syllable was defined as one containing a long vowel (like "slow") or diphthong (like "joy"), or one whose short vowel was separated by more than one consonant from the next vowel. Examples of the third group might include: "Held," followed by "as" or, in fact, any syllable; "let" followed by "me" or any other syllable beginning with at least one consonant. To the Greeks and Romans, such syllables counted as "long," whether or not a linguist would have been able to measure a consistent differential between them and the length of syllables defined as "short." All poetry of the classical period was written according to these conventions, and the audience understood them well enough to distinguish between good and bad examples.

There is another difference between classical meters and our own accentual-syllabic meter in English. Classical meters were *logoaedic,* that is, any given line always (with a few exceptions) contained more than one kind of foot. For example, the classical hexameter (the meter of the Homeric epics and the *Aeneid*) consisted of six feet, the first five of which could either be spondees or dactyls, the sixth always a spondee or a trochee. Lines containing fully six spondees were possible but extremely rare.

Apart from prescribing certain meters for the line, classical poetry devised several stanza forms that required a different pattern of feet for successive lines in the stanza. *Alcaics,* for example, first used by a sixth-century B.C. Greek named Alcaeus, follow the following metrical scheme in a four-line stanza:

Line one: x—∪—x—∪∪—∪ x
Line two: x—∪—x—∪∪—∪ x
Line three: x—∪—x—∪—x
Line four: —∪∪—∪∪—∪—x

In this notation, *x* stands for a syllable that can be either short or long. In practice, all the final *x*'s of a line sound long, regardless of the nature of the syllable, because of the pause coming at the line's end—unless the line is enjambed.

Despite extra requirements and restrictions of classical meter, many postclassical poets have attempted to adapt them to their own language. This was particularly true during the Renaissance, when classical civilization was used as the model for achievement in all the arts. Efforts to imitate went in two directions. Some poets tried to use quantity as the basis for meter in a modern language—for example, Antoine de Baïf in French and Philip Sidney in English. Others substituted stress for quantity while retaining the metrical patterns of classical lines and stanzas. The problem with using quantity as a metrical base in English is that we don't hear distinctions in syllable length clearly enough to catch any recurrent pattern in quantitative meters. It is only when poems are set to music composed so as to follow the durational pattern of classical meter that length registers with us metrically. Otherwise we don't hear it; so meters using quantity in English are *purely* conventional, not rooted in a linguistic reality.

On the other hand, when poets substituted *stress* for syllable length, they were using a linguistic basis for meter that could actually be heard; and this version of classical meter has appeared over and over again in poetry since the Renaissance. Here is a stanza from Tennyson's "Milton," written in alcaics:

> O mighty-mouth'd inventor of harmonies,
> O skill'd to sing of Time or Eternity,
> God-gifted organ-voice of England,
> Milton, a name to resound for ages;

The stresses of Tennyson's lines fall where classical alcaics require a long syllable—always allowing for optional substitutions as outlined above. His adaptation of the form is unusual in that it also tries to conform to the length specifications of classical meter.

Much more common in English poetry are imitations of *sapphics,* a stanza devised by the sixth-century B.C. poet Sappho. The classical schema for the stanza is as follows:

> Line one: $-\cup-x-\cup\cup-\cup-x$
> Line two: $-\cup-x-\cup\cup-\cup-x$
> Line three: $-\cup-x-\cup\cup-\cup-x$
> Line four: $-\cup\cup-x$

Again, the last syllable of each line will always in practice sound long, regardless of the nature of the syllable, except when a short syllable is enjambed onto the next line.

As with alcaics, most efforts to adapt this meter for English have simply substituted stress for quantity, producing logoaedic meters that we can actually hear. Because of the immense reputation of Sappho, many poets writing in English have been drawn to attempt poems composed in her stanza—among them, Fulke Greville, Thomas Hardy, Swinburne, and Ezra Pound. Here is the first stanza of Swinburne's "Sapphics":

> All the night sleep came not upon my eyelids,
> Shed not dew, nor shook nor unclosed a feather,
> Yet with lips shut close and with eyes of iron
> Stood and beheld me.

Swinburne has also attempted here, in the majority of instances, to make syllable length coincide with syllable stress, so that the poem would conform to the demands of quantitative meter as well as metrical practice based on stress. Still, we would have to note that syllables like "and" or "with" (when followed by another consonant), though short in English pronunciation, in the classical system would not qualify as short because of multiple consonants intervening between vowels in consecutive syllables. Both Tennyson and Swinburne seemed to have trod a middle path in attempting to satisfy demands of quantitative meter and stress meter. We can say that, in general, those instances in which length *and* stress coincide are the most effective metrical adaptations of the older system. On the other hand, they are enormously difficult to achieve and have been described as "dancing in chains." Even in poems where no effort is made to take length into account, we can usually catch a difference in the handling of meter. Consider a stanza from Marilyn Hacker's "Going Back to the River," which is written in alcaics:

> I have a reading lamp and an open book.
> Last glass of wine, last morsel of St. André
>   prolong my dinner and my chapter
>   into the ten o'clock Haydn program.

I would introduce a note of caution, though, concerning the use of stress-level-2 accents. In line three above, "and" would always count as a stress in accentual-syllabic meter; here it fills in one of the stresses required by alcaics, but it is not as strong as the others in the line and thus risks not being heard. Also, the syllable "in-" in line four is at level 2 and might not be heard as a strong stress in this meter; the problem is aggravated by the presence of another syllable at stress level 2 ("clock"), which is meant to count as one of the line's weaker stresses. These intermediate stresses raise a doubt about the metrical pattern, a difficulty that wouldn't be present if we were dealing with ordinary accentual-syllabic verse. That doubt is probably sufficiently strong for us to introduce the following principle: When applying the metrical template of classical meters for poems using stress as the metrical base, it is safer to use only stress levels 1 and 3, to make certain that quantitative meter's unaccustomed patterns will register on ears not conditioned to hear them. Furthermore, if long syllables can also be made to coincide with strong stresses, and short syllables with weak stresses, the pattern will unfailingly make itself heard. True, doing so is difficult and may interfere with other desirable qualities we expect in a poem, but for some poets metrical challenges act as a stimulus to invention, so the results just possibly might justify the effort. Anyone curious to gauge the success of such poems might look for Marilyn Hacker's "Days of 1987" (sapphics), James Merrill's "Arabian Night" (sapphics), and my own "Remembering Mykenai" (alcaics) and "Sapphics at a Trot."

9. Syllable-Count Verse

Accentual-syllabic meter counts both the number of stresses and syllables in each line; but, as we noted in an earlier chapter, the Romance languages use only the number of *syllables* per line as the basis for their meters, disregarding stress altogether. The eleven-syllable line is the most frequent meter in Italian and Spanish poetry, as the ten- or twelve-syllable line is in French. A surprising development in the modern period was the adaptation of syllable-count meter for English and American poetry, which had before then always used stress as the primary metrical base. What led to this innovation? Partly it was the result of the high regard that English and American poets felt for French poetry during the last decades of the nineteenth century. If French poetry used syllable-count meter, then English-language poets hoping to appropriate some of its strengths would use it also.

Meanwhile, the French themselves had discovered Japanese poetry through new translations that began to appear in the 1880s and were stimulated by these to imitate Japanese forms—in particular, the haiku. There already existed a metrical similarity between French and Japanese poetic traditions, based on a shared linguistic feature in their languages. French language stresses only the last syllable of any phrase or sentence; stress is a marker of syntactic divisions, not a phonemic feature intrinsic to each word. Nor does Japanese language mark permanent stress differences among the syllables of a phrase or sentence; these vary according to context. So it is no surprise if both French and Japanese poetry use syllable-count as the basis for their meters. The basis for an affinity between the two poetries existed even before the West began to establish trade relations with Japan.

As English and American poets became aware of late-nineteenth-century French poetry, they also came to know the new translations from Japanese and discovered in these as well a metrical principle different from the accentual-syllabic meter of their own tradition. The wish to experiment with that principle resulted in the earliest syllable-count poems in English.

Suppose we look at particular examples of this meter. The *haiku*, for example, is a three-line Japanese poem with a five-syllable first line, a seven-syllable second line, and a five-syllable last line, bringing the poem's total to seventeen syllables. The form makes no provision for the distribution of stresses in each line; they fall where they may, just so long as the first line has five syllables, the second, seven, and the third, five. In this very small poetic space, condensed visual presentation can convey whole realms of emotion and intuition, as in this haiku of Bashō's:

> Within the gold screen
> An old pine stands motionless—
> Alone in winter.

These seventeen syllables call up in our minds a sharply outlined vignette: a person, probably a man (and perhaps Bashō himself), is at home in winter looking at a familiar screen standing in his room. The warmth of that familiar screen contrasts with the age of the pine (which probably finds a counterpart in the age of the observer). On the one hand, the brilliant gold background of the

screen; and, on the other, an ancient pine and the observer's soli-
tude, a solitude underlined by winter bleakness. Haiku itself is
rather like a photographic slide projected on a screen, an instan-
taneous "take" on reality that allows for a kind of contempla-
tion associated with Buddhism: the moment is eternal and the
moment is also an illusion. It is transitory but filled with time-
less awe.

One convention of haiku we can note in this poem is that
somewhere in its three lines an indication of the season must
appear—in this case, winter. The Japanese term for the season-
al word is *kigo,* which need not actually name the season so long
as some natural marker for it is given; for example, cherry blos-
soms always stand for spring, and red maple leaves, for autumn. A
strong connection between haiku and the natural order is implied,
and most haiku deal with nature rather than life in towns or cities.
The season is always of course more prominent when experienced
outdoors than within the shelter of a human dwelling; moreover,
there are "seasons" in a human life, from springlike youth, to win-
try old age. In Bashō's poem, we can sense the thoughts of an old-
er practitioner of the art of haiku as he contemplates the occasion
of vision at a point late in his life. Instead of merely conceding
to the wintry ravages of time, he makes them the subject of the
poem, which is a way to redeem them at least partially. The respect
Bashō accords to the ancient, solitary pine returns in the respect
the reader might accord to both the tree and the poet.

The haiku came fairly late to Japanese poetry, developing out
of an earlier form known as *renga,* a five-line form with syllable-
count as follows: 5, 7, 5, 7, 7. The first three lines were usually con-
sidered a main subdivision, followed by the final two. *Renga* was

a joint venture in composition, usually involving three poets, who supplied in turn either the opening three-line section or the concluding couplet. Each addition had to relate to its predecessor, though not necessarily to anything before that, so the *renga* skipped merrily about from thing to thing with only a general kind of unity, and normally concluded at one hundred lines. We can see that the haiku has the same syllable-count as the *renga*'s first three lines. Beginning in the fourteenth and fifteenth century, some poets wrote poems by detaching the three-line section as a complete unit in itself. This became very popular in the seventeenth century, when Bashō and several other poets brought the form to a high degree of perfection.

Apart from haiku, the first codified form in English to use syllable-count as its metrical base was the *cinquain,* a form invented by an American poet named Adelaide Crapsey. Her cinquain had (as we might guess from the term) five lines, the syllable count as follows: 2, 4, 6, 8, 2. The relationship to the *renga* stanza is obvious, but Crapsey used even numbers of syllables in her lines, which allowed for the occasional introduction of regular iambic meter into the poem. Actually, any line in English poetry that contains an even number of syllables tends to gravitate toward iambic meter because of the nature of our language and its poetic tradition. For that very reason, later practitioners of syllabic verse have tended to favor lines with odd-numbered syllable count, so as to move away from overly familiar iambic patterns. One of the theoretical justifications offered for poems using syllable-count meter was that they provided relief from the monotony of iambic insistence in English poetry.

In one form of syllable-count verse all the lines have the *same* number of syllables, a mode termed *isosyllabism* (or *isosyllabic verse*). An early example is Robert Bridges's long poem *The Testament of Beauty*, every line of which contains twelve syllables. Later examples include "Atlantis" by W.H. Auden, composed of seven-syllable lines, or John Hollander's book-length poem *Powers of Thirteen*, in which every line contains thirteen syllables. Isosyllabic verse is less common than what is termed *heterosyllabic verse*, syllable-count poems containing lines of prescribed but *differing* numbers of syllables. A poem may alternate between two totals in the syllable-count of its lines as it does in Auden's "A New Year Greeting," where eight-syllable lines alternate with seven-syllable lines. There are other possibilities: the poet may establish a special stanza in which a prescribed number of syllables is assigned to each line in a stanza, and the metrical template thereby established applied uniformly throughout the remainder of the poem, as in Marianne Moore's "The Steeple-Jack." Here, each of the poem's thirteen stanzas has six lines, and the syllable-counts of those lines are, respectively, 11, 10, 14, 8, 8, and 3. Such poems end up looking like one of George Herbert's heterometric poems, and he (along with the haiku and Crapsey's cinquain) may indeed have been Moore's partial model; but Herbert's poems are written in accentual-syllabic meter while Moore's lines count syllables only and not accents. Here is "The Steeple-Jack"'s first stanza:

> Dürer would have seen a reason for living
> in a town like this, with eight stranded whales
> to look at; with the sweet sea air coming into your house

on a fine day, from water etched
    with waves as formal as the scales
on a fish.

Besides changing the syllable count in these lines, Moore indents lines two and five, not because they have the same syllable count but because these two lines rhyme, as others in the stanza do not. Even in her unrhyming syllable-count poems, Moore often marks differences of indentation, probably in order to arrive at stanza shapes with a special visual appeal. Syllable-count verse's potential for forming arresting patterns on the page has led a number of poets after Moore to adopt her approach—in particular, Richard Howard in poems of his such as "1876."

Critics of syllable-count verse say that it has a visual function only and that individual lines do not register in our hearing as lines at all. They remark that we aren't conditioned to count syllables as we hear them, and that syllabic poems lack regularly recurring stresses that would cooperate to establish an auditory principle of lineation. In the Romance languages before the modern period, line endings were nearly always marked by rhymes, a feature that served to establish the line. Neither the haiku nor cinquain used rhyme, nor do most contemporary syllable-count poems. On the other hand, some modern syllable-count poems do use it—for example, Moore's "The Fish," a poem that rhymes four of each stanza's five lines. In this way Moore signals where those lines end, even without the assistance of a regular pattern of stresses.

A reckonable percentage of Marianne Moore's poems do not

rhyme, though, and lines in her unrhymed poems are hard to perceive without the assistance of the printed page. The sense of line for some poets is a less important unit than the syntactic unit, the sentence, or the verse paragraph. We've already noted that Moore regarded the punctuated syntactic unit her primary measure, whereas her syllable-count stanzas were arranged as such for their purely visual appeal. The practice no doubt arises from an inescapable fact: The audience for contemporary poetry comes in contact with the text most often via the printed page. If, under syllable-count governance, a strong impression of recurrent pattern is lost, what *is* gained is a rhythmic variety of the kind usually reserved for conversational speech, and, along with that, the chance to design arresting visual shapes in lines of differing length. Some poets, Richard Howard among them, would argue that the visual appeal of heterometric syllable-count poems sufficiently justifies them. And some would also note that, even with isometric syllable-count poems (in which stanzas take quite ordinary shapes), the purely arbitrary restriction of adhering to a fixed number of syllables per line is an obstacle just difficult enough to help the poet toward more interesting second or third thoughts—in short, an artificial boost to the compositional process. If it is that, perhaps the reader can respond to syllable-count verse with a scratch of the head and a tolerant "OK, whatever helps you get the poem written."

Meanwhile, syllable-count verse can also exhibit qualities of composition by line available to both accentual-syllabic verse and free verse. There is no reason that a poem using the syllable-count principle may not include an occasional stretch of iambic meter.

Moore's "The Steeple-Jack" does so in the example quoted above, where the fifth line *could* be scanned as perfectly regular iambic tetrameter, a rhythmic detail that helps reinforce the idea of formal regularity in the fish-scale pattern described. There is, nevertheless, a problem connected to trying to hear some of the lines in syllable-count poems as accentual-syllabic. While standard accentual-syllabic meter guarantees that syllables at stress level two will count as accented syllables, syllable-count verse does not. Taking the line "with waves as formal as the scales" cited above, we can see that, in conversational speech, only the syllables "waves," "form-," and "scales" would be perceived as bearing a stress; the second "as" would not. And ordinary conversational word-stress is the norm throughout Moore's poem. In recordings of her poetry, however, Moore does mark a two-level stress on such syllables, so it is clear that, consciously or unconsciously, she worked with iambic meter as an occasional resource brought into syllable-count verse. To make doubly certain that interpolated iambic feet will register as such, poets will have better luck if they use only 1-3 iambs, and not rely on 1-2 or 2-3 iambs to make up the line.

On the other hand, if we grant the validity of free verse and agree that lines written without meter can be rhythmic and memorable, there's no reason that lines in syllable-count poems can't have the same kind of vigorous rhythmic pulse as lines in free verse. The author has added an extra restriction, the maintenance of a fixed syllable count; but that restriction won't prevent resourceful poets from arriving at good lines, and, as was already suggested, may actually help them do so by leading to more interesting second or third thoughts. Any poet using the system will have to keep in mind that individual lines, apart from maintaining the adopted syllable count, should have the linear coherence readers have come to expect; otherwise the syllable count won't seem a sufficient justification for the poem's line divisions. While we may allow that for some poets the sentence or verse paragraph is the compositional unit rather than the line, we also have to observe that most readers expect lineation to have a basis in sound, and so they will be disappointed if they can't discover that basis.

The same expectations concerning enjambment in metered poetry apply as well to syllable-count verse: there must be an expressive justification for an enjambed line apart from the purely arithmetical requirement of terminating a line when the syllable count has been reached.

Given the auditory conditioning we have acquired from the tradition of metered poetry in English, accentual-syllabic meter is the easiest way, of course, to give individual lines unity and inevitability; syllable-count meter has to devise other means. In practice, this involves paying close attention to stresses present in the line, even though they do not recur in regular patterns. It also demands close attention to the consonant and vowel sounds of the words present in a given line. Auditory concerns here are precisely the same as those confronting the poet writing in unmetered poetry (or *free verse*). In fact, no one can write syllable-count verse well who is not also able to compose good *un*metered poems. It's also possible to argue that no one in the contemporary period can write good metered poetry (poetry that, despite its regular meter, has the requisite fluidity and variety of conversational speech) who does not also understand the tradition of unmetered poetry that has been practiced now for just over a hundred years.

10. Unmetered Poetry

Poetry without a regularly recurring numerical principle in its rhythmic construction is usually called *free verse,* a translation of the French phrase *vers libre,* though a more exact translation would be *free line.* For over a hundred years experimental poets have written free verse—in its early phase, a consciously chosen departure from traditional prosody, but now so widespread and automatic that many free-verse practitioners are almost entirely without knowledge of the earlier system. Accounting for free verse's increasing importance in Western literature over the last one hundred years is beyond the scope of this manual; but we can at least make a quick sketch of free verse's origins, which is one way of understanding what it is.

The *vers libre* concept was first advanced by Gustave Kahn, a late-nineteenth-century French poet. His precedents were, first of all, the prose poem that had been developed during the French Romantic period, and then Rimbaud's unmetered poems in *Les Illuminations.* Rimbaud's poems were written in the early 1870s but known only to the small audience who had read circulated manuscripts, which were not published and widely appreciated until more than a decade later. Kahn and several of his contemporaries began writing poems that dispensed with the strict rules of classical French prosody, and theoretical discussion of the new practice appeared during the mid-1880s in magazines like *La Vogue* and *La Revue Indépendante.* Translations of Whitman also appeared in these magazines, adding a foreign precedent for the new French practice. Kahn asserted that *vers libre* allowed for a closer fit between consciousness and expression; dispensing with traditional restraints allowed poets to find a more flexible verbal counterpart for elusive feelings—and to discover subtle rhythms that standard metrical practice would rule out. Logic could be replaced by the fluidity of free association, and a new sound would be brought into French poetry. *Vers libre* did not, however, immediately win many adherents, and its validity has never gone uncontested, despite its position as the dominant mode in French poetry of the twentieth century. Not even Paul Valéry, *vers libre*'s most persuasive antagonist, was able to dissuade the majority of practicing French poets from adopting it.

The history of free verse in English parallels its history in the sister language. During the last decades of the nineteenth century, partly because of the special international esteem accorded to French poetry, free verse found many imitators in England and America; but again, it hasn't been accepted by all poets or critics even to the present day. Nevertheless, English poetry had its own persuasive precedents for the new system, beginning with the rhythmically vigorous but unmetered King James Authorized Version of the Bible, especially its translations of the Psalms. Milton, while keeping to an iambic norm, varied line lengths at will in poems like *Lycidas* and *Samson Agonistes*. James Macpherson in his fabricated archaic poems by the imaginary bard "Ossian" used an irregular metric reminiscent of the Psalms or Milton. Martin Farquhar Tupper, an English popular sage, wrote a book titled *Proverbial Philosophy* (1838) in unmetered rhythmic versets, the form of which influenced Whitman when he was developing his own verse practice. For poetry written in English, Whitman is usually cited as the turning point from metered to unmetered poetry. Whitman's lines are famously long, and as such represent the trend of free-verse writing in English, which for the most part involves long lines, just as French *vers libres* are mostly short. Whitman's example influenced long-lined American poets like Sidney Lanier and Richard Hovey, as well as Stuart Merrill and Vielé-Griffin, who emigrated to France, wrote mostly in French, and participated in the development of *vers libre* in their adopted country.

In the early twentieth century, free verse's best-known proponents were Ezra Pound and T.S. Eliot. Eliot most often described his technique as *"vers libre,"* yet he was not content with the idea of a verse that was "free," since "free" might be taken to mean "haphazard." Perhaps he had quickly become bored with poor examples of free verse. In his essay "Reflections on *Vers Libre*," he said, "And as for the so-called *vers libre,* which if good is anything but 'free,' it can better be defended under some other label." In other words, freedom to be irregular didn't dispense the poet from considering rhythmic effects carefully; for any poem written with the ideal of art in mind, this requirement is self-evident.

We might go a step further than Eliot and question the term "verse" as well, since the connotations of that word are mostly negative, reserved for poems of little scope or importance. When we say, "Oh yes, so-and-so writes *verse,*" we aren't usually talking about the work of a serious artist. Ask any poet whether she or he would prefer to write "poetry" or "verse," and you'll see what I mean. It seems odd, then, to hear a defense of "free verse," which could be taken to mean "haphazard scribblings of no particular importance." Much warmer connotations surround the word "poetry," a word used as an honorific in many and various contexts. All told, to the term *free verse,* I prefer *unmetered poetry.* If we say we are writing *unmetered poetry,* the implication is that we are nevertheless acquainted with the body of poems written in syllable-stress meter, to which the new method has a discoverable relationship. Those who have made a close study of traditional prosody usually write better unmetered poems than those who haven't, acknowledging regular patterns by making intelligent departures from them.

Even Whitman knew the older system, and was capable of writing in iambic as his poems "O Captain! My Captain!" and "To a Locomotive in Winter" show. It's also interesting to note that the first line of "Song of Myself" is perfectly scannable as iambic pentameter, and that iambic movement appears from time to time in other sections of the poem:

> I celebrate myself, and sing myself,
> And what I assume you shall assume.

The second line could qualify as pentameter, too, if we describe it as having initial truncation, a stress-level-two accent on "And," and a trochee for its fourth foot. There is a risk, though, in proposing foot scansion of lines that are unmetered. Since no consistent pattern governs "Song of Myself" throughout, we have no yardstick to assure the alternating weak-strong accentuation characteristic of the iambic foot. As a result, readers will place stresses only according to conversational habits. If the second line cited above is spoken as in ordinary conversation, accents will fall on "I," "-sume," "you," and the second "-sume." That reading would still give us iambic tetrameter, with anacrusis and one trochaic substitution in the third foot. Making a survey of the lines coming after this one, we don't discern any regularly recurring pattern that would tell us whether to scan the line as tetrameter or pentameter. No scansion applied to the poem as a whole can go further than marking all the syllables that seem to receive stress at level three, and we don't find any consistent pattern in the results.

It's possible to imagine a prosody in which lines could all be scanned as a varying number of iambic feet, none of the feet composed of 1-2 iambs (or, for that matter, 2-3 iambs, which also make for doubtful scansion in *free verse*). In this prosody, substitutions and truncations could account for any divergence from an easily perceived iambic norm. Those experienced in iambic meter, however, know that lines composed entirely of 1-3 iambs are hard to achieve for long stretches, even apart from the question of whether meter achieved without intermediate accents wouldn't end up sounding overemphatic and dull. In any case, I know of no practitioners who have ever tried to dispense with 1-2 and 2-3 iambs throughout an entire poem.

On the other hand, there are many instances in which an occasional line of an unmetered poem could be scanned as composed entirely of 1-3 iambs. These lines sometimes serve an expressive purpose, introducing a metronomic regularity into a poem whose rhythms are elsewhere unclassifiable. Here is an example from Roethke's poem "Forcing House":

> Great cannas or delicate cyclamen tips,—
> All pulse with the knocking pipes
> That drip and sweat,
> Sweat and drip,
> Swelling the roots with steam and stench,

In a poem most of whose lines have irregular rhythms, we discover the line about pipes "That drip and sweat,| Sweat and drip," which is a series of 1-3 iambs, provided the comma and line break serve as a weak stress. The next line is also composed entirely of 1-3 iambs, with a trochaic substitution in the word "Swelling." The regular dripping of the pipes is indicated rhythmically here by the use of iambic feet, a pulse that is then transferred to the plant roots by something like osmosis.

The mixing of irregular rhythm and iambic meter is very common in poetry during the first sixty years of the twentieth century and might be characterized as the dominant prosody for that period. We can grasp the expressive possibilities in the abstract without referring to further examples. Just as poets using the older prosody often departed from regularity into irregularity as an expressive resource, poets writing unmetered poetry might vary from irregularity into *regularity* from time to time in order to create some special rhythmic effect or emphasize a line or phrase within the whole. The practice does require a run of 1-3 iambs, though, if the audience is to hear it clearly.

Rather than drawing a sharp boundary between metered and unmetered poetry, it makes more sense to establish a continuum or sliding scale, with metrical strictness at one end and rhythmic

indeterminacy at the other. In the twentieth century, strict pros-
ody continued to govern a reckonable percentage of the poetry
written in every decade—witness the poetry of Frost, Elinor Wylie,
Louise Bogan, Roethke, Lowell, Elizabeth Bishop, Weldon Kees,
Richard Wilbur, Anthony Hecht, Philip Larkin, Thom Gunn, W.D.
Snodgrass, James Merrill, Derek Walcott, Seamus Heaney, and on
up to the poets grouped under the heading "New Formalists":
Marilyn Hacker, Dana Gioia, Brad Leithauser, Mary Jo Salter, Gjer-
trud Schnackenberg, and Mark Jarman.

Meanwhile, works composed in the tradition of unmetered
poetry can be situated at varying distances from traditional prac-
tice. Some of these are quite close. For example, Edwin Arling-
ton Robinson, known primarily for poems in traditional meters,
wrote a poem titled "The Man Against the Sky," which can be
scanned as iambic, though line lengths vary from two to five feet,
stanzas have nonuniform lengths, and rhyming follows no set pat-
tern (even though every line is eventually rhymed somewhere in
the stanza). Here are a few lines from the poem:

> Whatever suns may rise or set
> There may be nothing kinder for him here
> Than shafts and agonies
> And under these
> He may cry out and stay on horribly

Again, stresses at level 2 (as on "for," "-nies," and "-ly") must be
counted in order to produce an unbroken run of iambics, just
as stress on the word "cry" must be demoted to level 2, in order
to provide the differential needed to produce the 2-3 iambic foot

"cry out." Robinson is consistent enough so that we can do this without being left in doubt about the line's scansion. Is this "unmetered poetry"? No, not entirely; but it doesn't follow a preordained pattern in the length of its lines, division into uniform stanzas, or the recurrence of rhymes.

Seeking more recent examples, if we turn to Robert Lowell's "For George Santayana," we discover that, though the poem's verse paragraphs vary in length, nearly every line can be scanned as iambic, with foot substitutions and the use of stress-level-2 accents. In fact, they can all be scanned as iambic pentameter, except for the last line, which is hexameter. In the first part of the poem, rhyme appears only sporadically, but the last six lines all rhyme. Do we call this "free verse"? Not quite: it is composed with the assistance of the old prosodic system, but it embodies a far from perfect regularity.

Moving further along the scale toward nontraditional versification, consider Lowell's "For the Union Dead." Here we find a less consistent use of iambic, lines of varying length, no rhymes at all, but nevertheless a division of the poem into a series of stanzas, each with four lines, one of which enjambs into the next stanza. The result is unmetered poetry, but it doesn't seem to deploy haphazard lineation and stanzaic division. Many of Lowell's poems fall into this gray area between traditional practice and entire deregulation, and the same can be said for Roethke, Berryman, and Elizabeth Bishop—plus a large number of poets coming after them. If we look at unmetered poetry being published now, the last vestige, apparently, of traditional prosody to be given up is regular stanzaic division. It's often true that contemporary poems with no iambic feet to speak of and lines of varying length will nevertheless divide the text into distichs, tercets, or quatrains. It's as though the poet were suggesting that some basic principle of quantification had been applied to the poem, even if an inaudible one. Without meter we have trouble hearing stanzaic divisions, especially when stanzas have been enjambed. If a poem keeps this vestigial metrical feature, it probably does so in order to invoke the mysterious power of number, which inspires unconscious respect in both poets and their audience. When poems are divided into uniform stanzas, spontaneous utterance is being made to encounter an abstract numerical principle, which lends something like magic or impersonal authority to the text.

At the opposite pole from unmetered poetry with a close relationship to standard prosody, we have contemporary poems with no relationship to number and meter at all. It's impossible, for example, to adapt traditional prosody to poems of e.e. cummings like "r-p-o-p-h-e-s-s-a-g-r," where lines are fractured and scattered over the page and even the individual letters of the word "grasshopper" are anagramatically rearranged into unpronounceable and therefore unmeasurable units. Cummings's poem exists primarily as a visual artifact. It isn't meant to be read aloud, and therefore it has no rhythm that can be quantified or analyzed. Some pages of Charles Olson's *Maximus Poems,* usually regarded as being composed according to the theories outline in his essay "Projective Verse," are nearly as unperformable as the cummings poem since fragments of text are disposed seemingly at random and indications of sequential order scant at best. With pages of this kind, the only means of taking in Olson's text is visual; our eyes skip around the page much as they do when looking at a painting. Without sequential connection between textual fragments, we have no run of syllables capable of being considered a sonic unit, and therefore no means of analyzing the poem's rhythm.

Less extreme but still unscannable is most of the poetry of William Carlos Williams, who took American speech rhythm and accentuation as the basis for his poetics, with constant enjambment acting as an interruption to a regular flow of patterned accents. Here is his poem "Tree and Sky":

> Again
> the bare brush of
> the half-broken
> and already-written-of
> tree alone
> on its battered
> hummock—
>
> Above
> among the shufflings
> of the distant
> cloud-rifts
> vaporously
> the unmoving
> blue

One characteristic of free verse immediately apparent is the presence of single-word lines: "Again," "hummock," "Above," and "vaporously" and "blue." Single-word lines are quite rare in the older prosody, partly because monometer is rare, as well as polysyllabic words that scan as more than dimeter. Unmetered poetry has the option of spotlighting single words under the full glare of attention we accord to a whole line. The question is always whether there is enough substance in a single word to bear that degree of attention. In Williams's poem, we notice that single-word lines are restricted to the opening and closing lines of the stanzas—with one midstanza exception, "vaporously" (or perhaps two, if "cloud-rifts" counts as a single word). Both stanzas (or verse paragraphs) contain seven lines. The opening lines—but no others—of stanzas are capitalized, even though the second ("Above") may or may not require capitalization, depending on whether it is regarded as completing the sentence in stanza one that ends in a dash. That dash is the poem's only punctuation; even the conclusion lacks a full-stop period. Notice also that both "Again" and "Above" are 1-3 iambs, if we scan them metrically. But "hummock" is a 3-1 trochee, and "blue" a monosyllabic foot, the only monosyllabic line in the poem. Perhaps the monosyllabic stress substitutes for full-stop punctuation. Syllable count of the lines runs from the minimum of one to the maximum of seven in line four, with all intermediate counts also present. Seven lines per stanza and seven different syllable counts are distributed over the poem: this conjunction cannot be accidental. Several lines of the first stanza end in at least consonants that rhyme ("n" and "f"), and the conclusion features a half-double rhyme, "unmoving" and "blue." Considering all these factors, we may call the poem "free verse" or "unmetered poetry," but it is certainly not haphazard. Williams had to lay his plans carefully in order to arrive at this short poem with its peculiar, reflective aura. Single-word lines and constant enjambment force us to slow down our reading speed, which tends to lend gravity and strangeness to the unpunctuated phrases.

In fact, "strong" enjambments are a feature of free-verse practice throughout the century, with many lines ending in definite or indefinite articles, as was almost never done in earlier poetry. The effect is of constant, breathless anticipation of the next line. Whereas in the older prosody, the line's most important word usually was the last word (an importance reinforced by rhyme), in unrhymed free verse, the line's most important word is generally the first (or second, if the first word is an article). Lines in free verse often make strong entrances and offhand exits—crescendo-diminuendo. This feature is more characteristic, however, of short-lined free verse than of long-lined. If pressed for a definition of *short-lined free verse,* I would call short-lined free verse any with average syllable counts up to nine—after which it becomes *long-lined free verse.*

For an example of the latter, let's look at Whitman's "Others May Praise What They Like":

> Others may praise what they like;
> But I, from the banks of the running Missouri, praise
>   nothing in art or aught else,
> Till it has well inhaled the atmosphere of this river,
>   also the western prairie-scent,
> And exudes it all again.

Note that the poem has only four lines, beginning with the capitalized words "Others," "But," "Till," and "And." Lines two and three are too long to be printed without an overrun, but they were composed as an unbroken line. The opening and closing lines of the poem have seven syllables each; the second line has twenty, and the third, twenty-two. We may ask ourselves whether lines two and three really can be experienced as single lines: they seem very long, and we may be tempted to break them into two parts. Try the experiment: make a new line at "praise" and another at "also." This lineation is plausible and yet—something is lost. The newly made line "Also the western prairie-scent" seems especially inadequate as a line, and much of the poem's impetuosity has been tamed. We are forced to conclude that Whitman's extremely long lines are intrinsic to his rhythmic sense and the intended effect of the poem. If we mark the stresses at level 3, we will discover the rhythmic units that look like iambic or anapestic meter for brief stretches in the line. But they are not carried through consistently; they register on the ear as transient rhythmic effects gauged by rule of thumb, not by any overall plan. The lines are nevertheless too rhythmic to sound like prose; they are lines of unmetered poetry, managed with skill and subtlety.

At the risk of overemphasis, I will state once more that there are many kinds of unmetered poetry, some close to the older practice, some far from it. Charles O. Hartman's *Free Verse, An Essay on Prosody* is a good survey of the different kinds of unmetered poetries that were developed by twentieth-century authors. However, since *free verse* by its very nature resists codification, Hartman's assertions, though reasonable, are hard to prove on the basis of texts alone. To take one example, I have heard some authors of free verse read enjambed lines in their poems without a pause, much as is done with enjambed lines in metered poetry; others

(Robert Creeley in particular) pause, even after "a" or "the." Without the benefit of audio reproduction, how can we be certain we are performing the lines as the author intended them to be heard? This is a good argument for the practitioners of unmetered poetries far removed from traditional prosody to include a note in each book giving the reader some idea how to read the poems aloud. No one seems to have done this, and the only assistance we have now comes from taped readings by those poets well known enough to have been recorded.

Poetry without meter wasn't always universally accepted even in the twentieth century—its most famous American opponent Robert Frost, who compared free verse to playing tennis without a net. Arguments for and against it have been presented clearly by Timothy Steele in *Missing Measures: Modern Poetry and the Revolt Against Meter*. Pound's often quoted recommendation to "compose in the sequence of the musical phrase, not in the sequence of the metronome" sounds persuasive but ignores the incommensurability of musical rhythm and verse rhythm. Eliot also said, "Any line can be divided into feet and accents," and this is probably too optimistic, not only because of extreme examples from cummings and Olson mentioned above, but also because scansion of a given line can often go more than one way; without a consistent yardstick the scansion remains undecidable. In an earlier chapter we saw that the line "When to the sessions of sweet, silent thought" could be read as though composed in more than one kind of metrical foot. It might be dactylic tetrameter, with final truncation, or, again, it might be iambic pentameter with an initial trochee, a 1-2 iamb for its third foot, and a 2-3 iamb in its fourth foot. In free verse, there is no prevailing yardstick capable of measuring individual lines.

Even if we decide to mark accents in free verse only where they fall in conversational speech, we must acknowledge that conversational habits differ according to individual speakers. Authors of free verse poems are forced, then, to accept that particular readers' accentuation of their poems will probably not correspond exactly to their own. Hopkins and Berryman foresaw this problem and added accent marks to syllables that might not be stressed in an impromptu reading; but the practice can be distracting, an intrusive affectation.

On the other hand, some authors may not mind that accentuation in their lines is indeterminate, no more than they mind that readers often bring a *conceptual* interpretation to the poem the authors never intended. Both issues involve questions in aesthetic theory: to what degree is the experience of the work the same for artist and audience; and how much control over the audience's experience should the artist try to exercise? I raise these questions here without, of course, resolving them. Meter or the lack of it is only a small test case in a much larger debate over the nature of artistic experience and the controls that define it.

To those who disallow unmetered poetry, no doubt the best answer is the achievement of poets who have written well in it. Anyone who dismisses free verse is also dismissing Whitman's "Song of Myself," Stevens's "The Snow Man," Eliot's *Four Quartets,* Williams's "The Yachts," Marianne Moore's "An Octopus," Auden's "Musée des Beaux Arts," Langston Hughes's "The Negro Speaks of Rivers," Lowell's "My Last Afternoon with Uncle Devereux

Winslow," Bishop's "At the Fishhouses," Plath's "Words," Ber-
ryman's *Dream Songs,* Anthony Hecht's "Rites and Ceremonies,"
Thom Gunn's "Bringing to Light," James Merrill's "An Urban
Convalescence," John Ashbery's "Self-Portrait in a Convex Mir-
ror," Amy Clampitt's "Beethoven, Opus III," Derek Walcott's "The
Fortunate Traveller," Adrienne Rich's "Transcendental Etude,"
and Seamus Heaney's "North." The point of orthodoxy (which
means "right opinion") has always been to guarantee consen-
sus among large numbers of adherents, but an orthodoxy that
excludes these and other poems of equal excellence from the can-
on will only seem attractive to a very small minority.

In free verse's favor is its imposition of little restraint on the
process of direct utterance. Language can be caught at its most
spontaneous, with the implication that unconscious forces were
more important in producing the poem than conscious ones.
Strained syntax, words chosen for rhyme alone, padding out of
lines so as to fill out the metrical count, or undue cutting away at
the natural texture of speech can be avoided. The implicit stance
behind every unmetered poem is that the author found this par-
ticular form of expression under no other constraints than the
desire to follow where feeling and expression led, without bow-
ing to preconceived, abstract formats devised in earlier eras and
under a differing set of conditions from those that gave rise to
the present poem. This comes close to saying that imposition of
abstract form on a poem always comes at the cost of entire sin-
cerity or authenticity.

Sincerity and authenticity themselves are not, however, easily
defined or achieved, in life or in literature; Lionel Trilling wrote

a thoughtful book on the subject that deserves rereading. In any case, no reader of the body of poetry in English can really believe that traditional prosody has always been a barrier to sincere or authentic speech. Denying that it remains an available resource in modern poetry requires dismissing Frost's "Design," Robert Penn Warren's "Bearded Oaks," Auden's "The Shield of Achilles," Lowell's "The Quaker Graveyard in Nantucket," Bishop's "One Art," Wilbur's "Walking to Sleep," Larkin's "The Whitsun Weddings," Hecht's "The Book of Yolek," Thom Gunn's "The Man with Night Sweats," Merrill's "Santorini: Stopping the Leak," Derek Walcott's "Beachhead," Seamus Heaney's "Glanmore Sonnets," Clampitt's "A Procession at Candlemas," and most of the poetry of Marilyn Hacker, Dana Gioia, Mary Jo Salter, Brad Leithauser, and Gjertrud Schnackenberg.

It may be useful to sum up the disadvantages of both approaches, beginning with metered poetry. First, we must concede that even with metered poetry we can't always know for certain where stresses fall. Given that experts differ in their scansions of particular metered poems, it's obvious that authorial control of reader performance is never absolute even when traditional prosody is being used. A second problem has to do with the incompatibility of the demands of traditional prosody and one of the modern period's central aesthetic absolutes—that the language of poetry conform to English as it is actually spoken. In earlier centuries poets could use inverted syntax ("I could not love thee, dear, so well| Lov'd I not honour more") and "poetic" contractions like "e'er," "o'er," and "e'en," or "th'unnumbered" to compose their iambic lines and place their rhymes. A special "poetic" diction is now forbidden, and inversion condemned as pointless self-deformation. Without these metrical conveniences, it has become harder for practicing poets to write within the rules of traditional prosody than in earlier centuries. If we turn to the issue of rhyming, we have to take into account the problem of English's overall scarcity of good rhymes—the good ones, after centuries of use, already familiar and a bit tired. For some readers, the modern substitutes of variant or approximate rhymes, introduced for novelty and variety, actually grate on the ear and mar the poem. Then too, the insistent stresses of accentual-syllabic meter are always present in the background of attention and, because of their focused regularity, may usurp attention and distract the reader from what is being said. (This argument ignores the best metrical practice, in which meter is constantly varied by foot substitution and the use of 1-2 and 2-3 iambs.)

To those who value meter purely as a "framing" device, setting poetry apart from ordinary speech, opponents of meter would say that there are other, less insistent frames, like lineation and the use of blank space in a text, and that meter's function in that regard is redundant.

Returning to the sincerity and authenticity criterion, some authors have testified that the necessity of conforming to the metrical grid prevented them from saying exactly what they wanted to say with the freshness of expression in which it had first come to them, and that they prefer freshness to metrical regularity. A few free verse advocates, giving an ideological coloration to the adjective "free," see the use of traditional prosody as part of a stance that involves political repression or at least an imposition of a numbing decorum on liberated, spontaneous consciousness and action. Connected to the two previous objections is the complaint that meter's familiar rhythm blocks subtler rhythmic effects available to the practitioner of free verse. And, finally, some authors see the use of meter as a form of cultural nostalgia, a refusal to take up the task of innovation that characterizes any living art.

Meanwhile, here are the problems most often cited concerning the practice of free verse. As already noted, the placing of stresses becomes mostly indeterminate for readers, who will remain in doubt about the author's rhythmic intentions and will therefore be unable to grasp the complete meaning of the poem. Poetry is sometimes defined as "memorable speech," and certainly it is a pleasure to say poems from memory; but unmetered poems are much harder to memorize than metered ones.

The next disadvantage is from the standpoint of composition: when writing the poem, the author has to create each line from scratch, deciding what the play of stresses is to be and where the line ends. (Whereas, if you write a ballad, for example, those decisions are made in advance; iambic tetrameter must alternate with iambic trimeter and lines two and four rhyme.) In art, whenever there is actual choice, the artist must choose with expressive intent; there should be communication in all aspects of what the artist chooses to offer the audience. The free-verse poet is confronted at every point with an almost unlimited number of possibilities, with the resulting necessity, at every point, of making technical decisions. The burden of constantly inventing new means of communication may be so great as to make it impossible to continue. If the poet decides *not* to make a conscious decision at points where choice is available, and so manages to complete the poem, the result may leave an impression of arbitrariness, as though technical aspects were handled with no forethought or expressive finesse. Then the reader will conclude that the poem would be no more and no less effective if the lineation were different and stresses fell at other points in the line—and will wonder why it isn't simply blocked out as prose.

In those cases in which the free-verse poet *has* brought conscious invention into every feature of rhythm and lineation, the task of reading becomes more complicated since it involves troubling to discover (or guessing) why lines end where they do, or stresses fall where *they* do. The whole interpretative task becomes that much more laborious. (This is still preferable to reading poems in whose sound there is nothing to interpret.)

To expand on Frost's objection about "playing tennis without a net," free verse is often experienced as being too easy. It doesn't offer the affirmative pleasure of (as Wordsworth said) the "sense of a difficulty overcome." Writing an Italian sonnet is hard. When a poet manages it well, the audience experiences a sense of vicarious pride in what human abilities and effort are capable of doing, and this becomes a model for other kinds of challenges that can be taken on and mastered outside the realm of art. Some would even go on to say that unmetered poetry suggests a lack of discipline, an unwillingness to work within reasonable guidelines, and that, as a model for behavior, it fosters unreliability, since the reader is never given any norm to gauge performance by and therefore never knows what to expect next.

To return to purely literary values, it has also been said that unmetered poetry actually erodes individual style, that all free verse sounds alike, while the presence of an abstract grid as a background actually spotlights differences in the individual voices of poets. As for the objection that the speech-norm now applied to poetry makes it too difficult for poets to compose in meter and rhyme, it has to be acknowledged that some poets have managed to write within the old restrictions and still achieve a speechly, conversational, sometimes even a slangy idiom. Nor does adopting the older system require a conservative politics, considering that a number of poets of liberal or left politics, like Bertold Brecht, Marilyn Hacker, or Tony Harrison (who writes in English working-class dialect), nevertheless use meter and rhyme. Finally, it is argued that without the presence of a living tradition of metered poetry, the audience will not bother to learn how to hear meter and so will no longer be able to achieve a complete understanding of poetry written in earlier centuries. Older poetry will then be accessible only to scholars, and perhaps not even fully accessible to *them,* as far as meter is concerned. A great artistic treasure trove will be lost to the present day.

Where do these bipolar objections leave us? If they leave us in the dark, perhaps it is at least a creative dark. The best answer to both sets of objections, as said earlier, is the body of excellent work done in each mode. Practitioners of metered poetry and free verse do well to be aware of the objections made to the mode they adopt, and to show, somehow, in their poems that they are doing all they can to overcome those objections. Those writing unmetered poetry might consider making recordings of all their poems, or offering notes on how particular poems are meant to sound. It is also possible that main conventions will eventually emerge in free-verse practice as time passes.

To repeat what was said above, a successful contemporary poem, written with or without the assistance of meter, will tend to weaken adversary arguments made in the abstract against its form. And there is no reason why a contemporary poet cannot write some poems in free verse and others with the assistance of traditional prosody. Readers with a strong ideology for or against either practice will dismiss the poems that don't support that ideology, but it's impossible to please all the people all of the time, and one advantage of writing poetry is that it offers an occasion, before all else, at least to please the author.

Selected Bibliography

I have been reading manuals and treatises on prosody for three decades, all of them no doubt leaving an impression, even when I no longer remember the titles or authors. Here are a few books and reference works that should set the student of prosody on the path to further discoveries about a topic that is practically inexhaustible.

Gross, Harvey, ed. *The Structure of Verse*. Revised Edition. New York: Ecco Press, 1979.

Gross, Harvey, and Robert McDowell. *Sound and Form in Modern Poetry*. Ann Arbor: University of Michigan Press, 1996.

Hartman, Charles O. *Free Verse: An Essay on Prosody*. Princeton: Princeton University Press, 1980.

Hollander, John. *Rhyme's Reason: A Guide to English Verse*. New Haven: Yale University Press, 1981.

Malof, Joseph. *A Manual of English Meters*. Bloomington: Indiana University Press, 1970.

Nabokov, Vladimir. *Notes on Prosody*. New York: Pantheon Books, 1964.

Pinsky, Robert. *The Sounds of Poetry: A Brief Guide*. New York: Farrar, Straus and Giroux, 1998.

Preminger, Alex, and T.V.F. Brogan, eds. *The New Princeton*

Encyclopedia of Poetry and Poetics. Princeton: Princeton University Press, 1993.

Saintsbury, George. *Historical Manual of English Prosody.* First published in 1910. Reprinted with an introduction by Harvey Gross. New York: Schocken Books, 1966.

Scott, Clive. *Vers Libre.* Oxford: Clarendon, 1990.

Shaw, Robert Burns. *Blank Verse: A Guide to Its History and Use.* Athens: Ohio University Press, 2007.

Steele, Timothy. *All the Fun in How You Say a Thing: An Explanation of Meter and Versification.* Athens: Ohio University Press, 1999.

Steele, Timothy. *Missing Measures: Modern Poetry and the Revolt Against Meter.* Fayetteville: University of Arkansas Press, 1990.

Turco, Lewis. *The Book of Forms: A Handbook of Poetics,* 3rd ed. Hanover, NH: University Press of New England, 2000.

Wimsatt, W.K. *Versification: Major Lanugage Types.* Modern Language Association, 1972.

Wright, George T. *Shakespeare's Metrical Art.* Berkeley: University of California Press, 1988.

Index of Terms

Index of Poets and Poems Cited

Note: All poem titles are listed under the author's name, not as individual entries.

Appendix: Sample Scansions

"Holy Sonnet," John Donne

```
  3     1   1    3      1      3     1   3   1   2
Death,| | be| not proud,| though some| have call| éd thee

  3    1   1     3    1     2    2   3   2  3
Mighty| and dread| ful,| | for| thou art| not so;

  1    3     1    3      2      3     1  2   1   3
For those| whom thou| think'st thou| dost o| verthrow

  2   3     2    3       1   3    1    3    2   3
Die not,| | poor Death,| | nor yet| canst thou| kill me.

   1    3     1    3       1    2    1    3    1   3
From rest| and sleep,| | which but| thy pic| tures be,

  2    3     1    3    1    3    2    3     1   3
Much plea| sure;| | then| from thee| much more| must flow,

  1    3    1   2    2    3    1    3    1  3
And soon| est our| best men| with thee| do go,

 3    1   1    3      1    3    1 3   1 2
Rest of| their bones,| | and soul's| deliv| ery.
```

     2   3   I 3   2   3   I   3   I   3

Thou'art slave| to fate,|| chance, kings,|| and des| perate men,

   I   3   I   3 I   3   I   3   I   3

And dost| with poi| son, war,| and sick| ness dwell,

   I   3   I   3   I   3   I   3   I   3

And pop| py'or charms| can make| us sleep| as well

   I   3   I 2   2   3   2   3   I   3

And bet| ter than| thy stroke;|| why swell'st| thou then?

    2   3   2   3   I   3   I 3 I 2

One short| sleep past,|| we wake| eter| nally

   I   3   I 3   I   3   3   2   2 3

And death| shall be| no more;|| Death,|| thou| shalt die.

DACTYLIC DIMETER

from "Eve," Ralph Hodgson

   3   I   I   3 I   I

Eve, with her| basket, was

   3   I I   3   I   2

Deep in the| bells and grass,

   2   I I   3   I   2

Wading in| bells and grass

```
3   1   1   3
Up to| her knees.
```

```
3   1   1   3   1   2
Picking a| dish of sweet
```

```
3   1   1     3   1   2
Berries and| plums to eat,
```

```
3   1   1   3   1   2
Down in the| bells and grass
```

```
3   1   1   3
Under| the trees.
```

ANAPESTIC TRIMETER

"Ah Sun-flower," William Blake

```
2   3     2       3   1   1   3
Ah Sun| flower!| | wea| ry of time,
```

```
1   3     1   1   3     1   1   3
Who coun| test the steps| of the Sun,
```

```
2   1   3   1   1     3     2   1     3
Seeking af| ter that sweet| golden clime
```

```
1     1   3   1   1   3     1   1   3
Where the trav| eller's jour| ney is done;
```

  I   I   3   2   I 3   I   I 3
Where the Youth| pined away| with desire,

    I   I   3   2 I   3   I I   3
And the pale| Virgin shroud| ed in snow,

  I 3   I   I   3   I   I 3
Arise| from their graves| and aspire,

    I   I   3   2   3   I I   3
Where my Sun-| flower wish| es to go.

TROCHAIC TETRAMETER

"Queen and Huntress," Ben Jonson

    3   I   3   I   3   I   3
Queen and| huntress,| | chaste and| fair,

    3   I   3   I   3   I   3
Now the| sun is| laid to| sleep,

    3   I   3   I   3 I   3
Seated| in thy| silver| chair,

    3   I   3   I   3   I   3
State in| wonted| manner| keep;

    3   I   2   I   3   I   3
Hesper| us en| treats thy| light,

3   1   3 1   2 1   3
Goddess| excel| lently| bright.

3   1   3 1   3   1   3
Earth,| | let| not thy| envious| shade

3   1   3   1   2 1   3
Dare it| self to| inter| pose;

3   1   3   1   3   1   3
Cynthia's| shining| orb was| made

3   1   3   1   3 1   3
Heaven to| clear| | when| day did| close.

3   1   3   1   3   1   3
Bless us| then with| wishéd| sight,

3   1 3 1   2 1   3
Goddess excel| lently| bright.

3   1   3   1   3   1   3
Lay thy| bow of| pearl a| part,

2   1   3   1   3   1   3   1
And thy| crystal-| shining| quiver;

3   1   2   1   3 1   3
Give un| to the| flying| hart

    3   I   3   I   3 I 3 I
Space to| breathe,|| how| short so| ever:

    3   I   3   I   3 I   3
Thou that| mak'st a| day of| night,

    3   I   3 I   2   I   3
Goddess| excel| lently| bright.

IAMBIC TRIMETER

"Stars, I have seen them fall," A.E. Housman

    3   2   I   3   I   3
Stars,|| I| have seen| them fall,

       I   2   I   3   I 3
    But when| they drop| and die

2   3   I 3   I 3
No star| is lost| at all

       I   3   I   3   2   3
    From all| the star-| sown sky.

I   3   I 3   I 3
The toil| of all| that be

       2   3   I 3   I   3
    Helps not| the pri| mal fault;

ɪ 3 ɪ 2 ɪ 3

It rains| into| the sea,

ɪ 3 ɪ 3 ɪ 3

And still| the sea| is salt.

About the Author

Alfred Corn is the author of nine books of poems, including *Stake: Selected Poems, 1972–1992*, which appeared in 1999, and *Contradictions*, which appeared with Copper Canyon Press in 2002. He has also published a novel, *Part of His Story*, and a collection of critical essays titled *The Metamorphoses of Metaphor*. A new collection of essays titled *Atlas: Selected Essays, 1989–2007* is scheduled with the University of Michigan Press for 2008. He has received Guggenheim and NEA fellowships, an Award in Literature from the Academy and Institute of Arts and Letters, a fellowship from the Academy of American Poets, and the Levinson Prize from *Poetry* magazine. For many years he taught in the Graduate Writing Program of the School of the Arts at Columbia and has held visiting posts at UCLA, the University of Cincinnati, Ohio State University, Oklahoma State, Sarah Lawrence, Yale, and the University of Tulsa. For many years a contributor to *The New York Times Book Review* and *The Nation*, he also writes art criticism for *Art in America* and *ARTnews* magazines. In 2001 Abrams published *Aaron Rose Photographs*, for which Corn supplied the introduction. In October 2003 he was a fellow of the Rockefeller Foundation's Bellagio Study and Conference Center, and for 2004–2005 he held the Amy Clampitt residency in Lenox, Massachusetts. In 2005–2006 he lived in London, teaching a course for the Poetry School, and one for the Arvon Foundation at Totleigh Barton, Devon. In 2007 he directed a poetry week at Wroxton College in Oxfordshire, and in 2008 he taught at the Almàssera Vella Arts Center in Spain.

The Chinese character for poetry is made up of two parts: "word" and "temple." It also serves as pressmark for Copper Canyon Press.

Since 1972, Copper Canyon Press has fostered the work of emerging, established, and world-renowned poets for an expanding audience. The Press thrives with the generous patronage of readers, writers, booksellers, librarians, teachers, students, and funders—everyone who shares the belief that poetry is vital to language and living.

Major funding has been provided by:

Anonymous (3)

Beroz Ferrell & The Point, LLC

Lannan Foundation

National Endowment for the Arts

Cynthia Lovelace Sears and Frank Buxton

Washington State Arts Commission

For information and catalogs:

COPPER CANYON PRESS
Post Office Box 271
Port Townsend, Washington 98368
360-385-4925
www.coppercanyonpress.org

Copper Canyon Classics re-presents essential, formative poetry texts in an affordable format. This book is set in Legacy Serif, a font designed by American type designer Ronald Arnholm after close study of Nicholas Jenson's 1470 Eusebius. Display type set in Reminga Titling, designed by Xavier Dupré. Book design and composition by Valerie Brewster, Scribe Typography. Printed at McNaughton and Gunn, Inc.

Copper Canyon
Classics